True Bucketfilling Stories

Legacies of Love

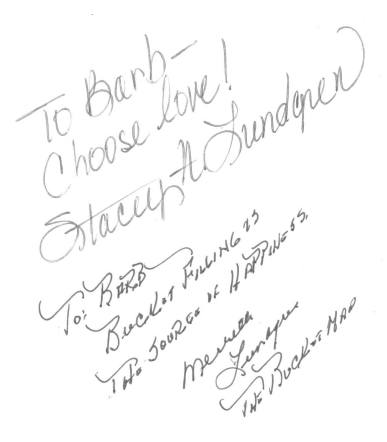

True Bucketfilling Stories

Legacies of Love

Stacey A. Lundgren

Peace Mountain Publishing, Inc.
HOWELL, MI

Library of Congress Card Catalog Number: 2009911973

ISBN: 978-0-9843366-0-9

Cover photo courtesy Ximagination, bigstockphoto.com

Typesetting, cover composition: Bellerophon Productions

Peace Mountain Publishing, Inc.
2112 Industrial Street
Howell, MI 48844
517.376.3090
info@peacemountainpublishing.com

Dedication

To Dad,

"The Bucket Man,"
with an abundance of
love and gratitude

Contents

Note to Readers

For many years I have been of the opinion that self-centeredness is one of the greatest evils of mankind, whether it is expressed by a nation, by a religion, or by an individual. These true stories represent people's choices to be other-centered rather than self-centered. This choice is an antidote to egotism and to the importance so many of us place on being "right"—being right at the expense of relationships and peace.

Hopefully, you will understand and forgive a father's pride in saying I believe this book to be important. My daughter, Stacey, is the author. But it is not only well-written, it contains a *vital message.* At the time of this writing, I am ninety years and five months old; I still go into classrooms and businesses and teach children and adults about bucketfilling; I've been doing this for 32 years. I realized at the age of 85, that perhaps I could not continue doing this work forever. It is both humbling and exciting to know that my beloved children, Stacey and Peter, not only continue in my footsteps, but take the truths of bucketfilling far beyond what I even imagined was possible. I am deeply gratified and grateful. My bucket is full!

Please . . . do not only read and enjoy these stories: take them into your hearts.

—Merrill H. Lundgren, "The Bucket Man"
October 2009

Acknowledgments

What a pleasure it is to thank the people who have given me love, support, encouragement, and inspiration as I took on this book project!

Mom and Dad, bless you. You have filled my bucket since the day I was born. Dad, special thanks go to you for your example, love, and leadership.

Love and appreciation go to Peter Lundgren, my brother and business partner, and Jill Kelbert, my compassionate and beautiful daughter. To my children, Justin, Rory Anne, Colton, and Kathryn, I am grateful to you for all you have taught me and for the myriad ways you have helped me to grow.

For the family of Bill Hulbert, my thanks and affection go to you for sharing Bill with us and, now, thousands of others.

Thank you to these people, too, for their great hearts and inspiration: James Vanover, Kristy Baggett, Elizabeth Fletcher-Brown, and Shellie Moore.

Craig Hines, my text and cover designer; Bob Land, my proofreader; and Dianne Morr, my editor—I appreciate you! Your expertise helped this project tremendously.

And now for you, my "serendipity friend" and mentor, Ed Helvey, thank you, thank you, and a big hug!

A special note of gratitude goes to the late Dr. Donald O. Clifton, who created the metaphor of the bucket and the dipper over 40 years ago.

Introduction

So, what is a bucketfiller? A bucketfiller is a person who lives his or her life with a warm and caring heart.

When my brother, Peter, and I were young, our parents took us to visit the salt mines beneath the city of Detroit. During the tour, the lights were turned off. It was pitch black. Not a pinpoint of light appeared anywhere. The man conducting the tour said that this was one of the rare places that is totally dark. Our eyes would not adjust so that we could see even a little bit, because there was absolutely no light. It was a strange experience. Sometimes I picture myself back there in that cold, dark mine, huddled with my family and other visitors. If I could have struck a match, I would have instantly been able to see the faces of those around me. I would no longer have felt alone or afraid. *Just one tiny flame could have done that.* Bucketfilling is similar. One act of bucketfilling (opening a door for someone, for instance) is like striking a match in a dark place. If others are bucketfilling at the same time, like smiling, reaching up to get something on a high shelf for a shorter person, or playing with a student on the playground who has no one to play with, those are *more* small flames. The more small flames there are, the more light there is to dispel the darkness.

We each have an invisible bucket. When it is full, we feel good—happy, peaceful, grateful, or loving. When it is empty, we feel bad—sad, lonely, angry, and frightened. Bucketfillers say and do nice things for other people. A bucket dipper is, of course, the opposite. A dipper might be mean, rude, self-centered, or in frequent bad moods. When we fill someone's bucket, we are filling our own at the same time. The same goes for dipping; when we dip in someone's bucket, we dip into ours.

We are all fillers and we are all dippers at various times during our lives. Hopefully, we are predominantly fillers. That, of course, is a choice. Bucketfillers bring light to our world, which, all too often, appears to be getting darker. My choice is to not focus on the darkness. Instead, we should all focus on bucketfilling by living our lives with warm and caring hearts.

The stories in this book are true. Most came from principals, teachers, and students in schools where we have presented our programs; several came from the lives of family members. A few of the stories began right before my eyes, and what followed was conveyed to me later. At the time, of course, I had no idea I would be preserving these simple, but profound lessons in a book. When did writing a book occur to me? When their power became apparent as I related the stories to others and tears came to their eyes. Then I realized that the stories could touch the lives of a much larger number of people if I simply wrote them down and created a book!

The bucketfilling lesson contained in each story is different from the others, yet they are certainly related. Each lesson demonstrates one or more positive impacts of bucketfilling. The "Let's Talk About It" questions at the end of each story encourage children and adults to talk about feelings, choices, and the joyful vibrations that bucketfilling acts continue to transmit around the world. How are your lives like the characters in these stories? Do you identify with any particular person? If yes, why? What did you learn from the bucketfiller(s) in this story? What did you learn from the bucketdipper(s)? Yes, we not only learn from bucketfillers but also the dippers.

My mother, now age 90, was a wonderful friend to me as I was growing up. When I came home from school and complained about this student or that student picking on me and being mean, she would hug me, smile, and say, "Stacey, even nasty people have an important purpose, so be grateful for them. They serve as bad examples to others." Do you know what? She was right! She has a great sense of humor and a basic wisdom that has helped me through many challenges during my lifetime. So, let's all remember to be *good* examples and fill the buckets of people we encounter throughout our lives. The undeniably natural result of that choice is that our own buckets will stay full. Now, I present these stories to you with my best wishes for a heartwarming and bucketfilling life.

S.A.L.

CHAPTER 1

The Homeless Shelter

We Can Choose to Refill Our Own Buckets

Tracy was in shock. Her husband of six years had told her this morning that he wanted a divorce. How could he want that? They had adopted three children together! These adoptions were the biggest and most challenging thing Tracy had ever done in her life. Now Paul said that he wanted out of the marriage and was moving with another woman to Hawaii. Hawaii? Hawaii was many hours away by plane. This obviously meant he wanted total separation. There would be no shared parenting. Tracy was losing her husband, and their children were losing their adoptive father. He packed two large suitcases and left immediately, even before the children got home from school. She had to break the news to them. What could she possibly say?

When Kathleen, Tory and Cody came home from school, Cody shouted, "MOM! We're going outside to shoot baskets!" And Cody and Tory were gone. Kathleen walked into the living room where Tracy was sitting quietly. "Mom? What's up? You look like you've been crying." Tracy tried to smile at her daughter, but she couldn't manage even a fake smile. "Kathleen, honey, would you please go outside and ask your brother and sister to come in? I want to talk with all of you about something."

"Uh-oh," said Kathleen as she headed toward the back door. "I think you got another call from the principal about Tory."

Tracy waited. She really had no idea what to say that would soften the hard truth. But they had to know. She heard them come into the house. They walked into the living room slowly and silently. Tory looked especially worried. She had been in trouble at school quite a few times for bad behavior, and she obviously thought this would be about her.

"Sit down, okay?" said Tracy. They sat lined up on the sofa across from her. "I have something to tell you, and it won't be easy. Not for any of us. But first, I want you each to know that I love you, and I will always be here no matter what."

How do I tell three orphaned teenagers that the father they always dreamed of having was abandoning them? Paul has been Kathleen's daddy for three years. Cody and Tory have been here for only three months! Tracy looked at the children, who stared at her. They looked scared, as if their security blanket was about to disappear. And perhaps it was. Tracy opened her mouth, not certain of the words she would say.

"Kids, I found out something this morning that made me cry. In fact, I've been crying most of the day. I didn't guess this would ever happen, but it has." Tracy drew a breath. "Paul is gone." The children gasped. Tracy rushed to say, "Oh, I don't mean he died! I'm sorry, I said that all wrong. I mean he left the family. He's going to Hawaii." She stopped talking.

"You mean on vacation?" asked Kathleen. "Hey, I've wanted to go to Hawaii for a long time! How come we don't get to go?"

Oh, boy, thought Tracy. *Now what?* "No, no it's not a vacation. He's moving there. Without us," answered Tracy. She could feel tears stinging her eyes, but she fought them back. Cody and Tory sat very still and stayed silent.

Kathleen started to cry. She shouted, "Well, this is stupid! Why would he get three kids and then just move away? What's his phone number? I'm going to call him. This is so stupid!" Kathleen ran upstairs and slammed her door so hard it shook the house.

Tracy looked at her two older children. Tory was 14 years old and had a troubled past. Cody was 13 and had already suffered abandonment and abuse. How would this affect them? How would adding one more tragedy to their young lives do anything but harm? "I'm so sorry, you two. I'm in shock."

Suddenly Tory stood up and screamed, "It's my fault! This is all my fault! I should have stayed in the orphanage! If you didn't have me, he wouldn't have gone away! I knew this would happen!" And she ran downstairs to her room, sobbing loudly.

Cody remained in the room with his new mother. He stared at Tracy. As he stared silently, Tracy saw tears begin to slide down his face. But he said nothing. She got up from her chair and sat down on the sofa next to him. Tracy put her arm around her son, but he stiffened and twisted away. Then she, too, began to cry.

The reality of Paul's absence had slowly been sinking in for two weeks. Tracy spoke to the three children about it as often as she could. She reassured them that this was not their fault; it had nothing to do with them. Tracy was tempted to tell them about the other woman, but she did not do that. They were angry enough already. She didn't want to make it worse.

The day she first mentioned the word "divorce," all three children ran outside and didn't return until it was almost dark. Tracy had been terrified that they, too, would run away. But she gave them some space, and they came home.

What troubled Tracy the most was how negative the family's energy had become. Of course, they were experiencing heartbreak; sadness is bound to hang around for a long while. But the fog of anger and fear had to lift if they were going to make it as a family. Tracy was now the sole leader, and locking herself into her bedroom every evening after dinner was not helping the children or her.

What could she do? After all, Tracy was a teacher of the bucketfilling concept. Of all people, she should know what to do! But nothing this awful had happened before. Her bucket and the buckets of her children were totally empty. How could they ever be filled again?

For two days Tracy focused, or tried to focus, on the idea: "When you fill someone's bucket, you fill your own. A bucketfiller lives his or her life with a warm and caring heart. We are all in control of our own buckets, and it is our responsibility to make sure they stay full." These are some of the things she had been teaching people every day. Now, at this most challenging point in her life, could she do what she taught to others?

The idea popped into Tracy's mind as she drove home from the store. She saw a man standing on a corner, holding a sign that read, "I will work for food." He looked like he hadn't shaven in a week and his hair was greasy and stringy. He held the sign in one hand, and the other held a leash with a small dog on the other end.

A homeless shelter! thought Tracy. *We'll volunteer at a homeless shelter!* Her children had been homeless, which is why they lived in orphanages. They could probably identify with some of what homeless adults and families go through. Even though things were terrible right now, perhaps filling the buckets of those less fortunate would lift their spirits.

Tracy made several phone calls to find out where they could help. Because they lived in a large city, there were several shelters that needed volunteer assistance. But the one that Tracy secretly hoped would not need them was the one that needed them most. She had passed it quite a few times when she was downtown; it was a rough-looking place. Long lines of men in raggedy clothes stood outside the shelter door for what Tracy assumed to be meals. She thought, *How could we help there, a woman with three teenagers, and two of them girls? Should I expose them to such a place?* Tracy decided they would do it, knowing she would watch each of the children closely.

The four of them began to spend time at the shelter on weekends, mainly in the kitchen and dining area. The cook, Max, was a homeless man who had been staying at the shelter for almost two months. In exchange for his lengthy stay, Max, a former professional chef, agreed to serve as cook at the shelter. He prepared breakfast and lunch for the four homeless men who were working and living at the shelter. But his main job was preparing a huge dinner for sometimes more than 150 homeless people who lined up daily, hours ahead of time, to get their only meal of the day.

The first time Tracy and the children were there for several hours felt awkward. They didn't know people's names or where things were kept, and Tracy was nervous about the children being out of her sight for more than a minute at a time. When they got into the car to go home, Tracy was relieved to be leaving. But the next time was easier, and each time they returned, they felt more comfortable.

The supervisor assigned their tasks; Tracy usually helped Max by cutting vegetables, peeling potatoes and slicing pies. Kathleen and Tory set the numerous tables for dinner and filled salt and pepper shakers. Cody carried heavy boxes of food and supplies from the huge cooler and storeroom into the kitchen.

Tracy chatted with Max as they worked; he opened up to her about his life. At 40 years old, he had lost his family because of his alcoholism and gambling. His wife had heard enough of his empty promises to get help. Max lost his job, the house and all their money. She divorced him. She and their three children moved in with her mother, and Max moved onto the streets.

"It happened so fast, I couldn't believe it. I always had a place to live and food to eat. Then all of a sudden I'm wandering the streets, missing my family, crying, always cold and tired. I was living a nightmare. I haven't seen my wife or children in over four years. She may have let me see the kids, but I was too ashamed to contact her. Now it's been so long, I'm afraid my kids wouldn't even want to talk to me."

Tracy asked him how long he'd been living in this shelter. "Six weeks now. It's the longest time I've spent in one place since I left home." Max shrugged his shoulders. "Hey, it's a bed to sleep in, I'm out of the weather, and most of the guys are okay."

In spite of his tough life, Max smiled a lot—a big toothy grin that was quite contagious. He expertly moved about the kitchen. At 6:00 P.M., Max told Tracy and the children to line up along the counter in the kitchen and start filling dinner plates. He then told a couple of the guys, "Okay, open the door and let the guests in!" and about 125 people, mostly men, filed into the dining room.

He calls them "guests," thought Tracy. She smiled to herself. *I like that.*

The guests in line shuffled along the other side of the counter, taking their plates as Tracy and the children worked in a speedy assembly line to fill them with spaghetti, salad and garlic bread. Most mumbled, "Thank you"; some looked intently, although briefly, into Tracy's eyes. She imagined they were silently asking, *Why are you here doing this? Are you judging me?*

Even a quick glance into their eyes told Tracy they held pain. She wanted to ask, *What is the story of how you got here?* But she remained silent and smiled as she handed them plates of food.

Cody, Tory, Kathleen and Tracy helped Max and the guys clean up after the guests had eaten and left. Some went upstairs to a shower and clean bed if they had signed up soon enough in the morning. But most went back outside to something else. Tracy did not know to what, but she guessed to sleep in the park or behind stores in alleys. For perhaps the first time in her life, Tracy felt deeply grateful for the things she and her children had, the simple things she took for granted. They would soon leave. They would climb into their mini-van and travel back to their clean home, where they would each go to sleep in warm beds, secure in the knowledge that they belonged somewhere and were safe. The next morning they would wake up knowing there was food for breakfast, friends at work and school, and that each member of their newly blended family was learning to love and trust one another.

Paul wasn't there, and that still hurt—it might hurt forever. But Tracy's bucket felt fuller. Instead of thinking about missing Paul as she fell asleep that night, Tracy thought of Max the Chef and hoped he would soon find the courage to contact his children. Perhaps his story, at least, could have a happy ending.

They returned to the shelter many times to fill buckets. Cody easily conversed with the various restaurant owners and grocers who delivered donated food, and when he unloaded huge boxes from their vehicles, he felt proud that he knew exactly where they should go. Tracy noticed that he was smiling again, something he hadn't done in a long while. Tory and Kathleen chattered away with each other and laughed as they went about their shelter chores. At home after Paul left, they had sprawled themselves on the sofa, glumly watching television. All of them had awakened during the night with bad dreams, and in the morning they felt grouchy and exhausted. But that was changing.

Losing Paul was something Tracy and her children did not choose. It was painful beyond description. But losing themselves would have been a choice. Instead of focusing on themselves and their pain, they chose to place their attention on something else: They spent hours giving to people who needed them.

As they drove home after their shifts, Tracy and the children talked about whom they had met and what they had learned that evening.

"Mom!" said Cody. "You know Spence?" Tracy had met Spence the first day they went to the shelter. He had been staying there for several weeks in exchange for work—a man about 30 years old. Tracy noticed over time how he and Cody had formed a friendship. She watched them as they worked together. They talked a lot.

Cody continued, "We were stacking boxes of carrots and stuff in the cooler and he says, 'You wanna see my foot?' So I said, 'What about it?'"

"And he said, 'I used to work for the circus, and one of my jobs was to feed the tigers. It was easy. I just walked in there, threw the meat to them, and walked out. So one day I walked into the cage in my bare feet. And WHAM! That tiger knocked me down and bit off half my foot. I went to screaming like crazy and a trainer fired a shot into the air and pulled me out of there.'"

"Oh, come on," said Tracy. "That can't be true."

"No, Mom, really! Spence said it really happened. So I said,

'Yeah, I wanna see your foot.' He pulled off his boot and sock, and there it was. It was awful, but it was cool." Cody was grinning from ear to ear. "He keeps two socks stuffed into the toe of his boot so he can walk without limping. I mean, his toes were just GONE. And half his foot, too. There were scars and everything."

"Wow!" Tracy said, looking at Cody's glowing face in the rearview mirror.

He kept talking. "And so he laughed and said to me, 'Hey, don't ever feed a tiger in your bare feet.' And then he said, 'Don't screw up your life with drugs, either. I was on cocaine for a long time, and probably if I hadn't been on it that day, I wouldn't have been so dumb. I got half a foot to remind me.' And he was smiling, Mom. He's really a nice guy. I wonder if he's homeless because of the drugs." Cody sat back in his seat and was quiet then.

Tracy wondered if he was thinking about Spence or Paul. But she guessed it didn't matter at that point. Spence had shared something valuable with Cody. He taught him something that perhaps a father should teach, but in the absence of a father, Spence filled an important void. He cared enough to do it, and Tracy felt grateful.

They spent five weekends working at the homeless shelter. Over that time, things changed in their family. *They* changed. The sadness over losing Paul was still there in the background, of course, but they had something new to think about, to talk about. Tracy and her children shared stories with each other about men they had spoken with at the shelter. Tracy told the children about Max. Cody told the girls and his mom about Spence several times. And the girls told Mom and Cody about Harry. Harry came to the shelter every Wednesday and Saturday to deliver baked goods that hadn't sold at his bakery the days before. Instead of throwing them away, he brought them to the shelter. He also enlisted a couple of large grocery stores to contribute their unsold baked goods, which he picked up. Thanks to Harry, there were plenty of donuts, cookies, pies and loaves of bread for the men to eat.

"Mom, Kathleen and I helped Harry again," Tory announced.

"Great. Did you do the usual?" *The usual* meant carrying in trays of desserts.

"Yes, but then something else happened."

"Like what?" Tracy asked.

"Well, there was a girl with him who was about Kathleen's age. And she was helping, too. It was Harry's daughter. Her name is Amanda, and this weekend was the first time she saw Harry *ever!*"

"EVER?" Tracy asked.

"Yes. He's been talking to her on the phone, but yesterday Amanda and her mom came into town. Did you know that Harry used to be homeless, Mom?"

"No, I didn't know that."

"Well, he did. His parents kicked him out of the house when he was 13! He lived with some friends, and then he was out on the streets. He even went to prison for a few years when he was older. I can't believe it! Harry is so nice."

Tracy understood why Tory was surprised. She knew that several of the men at the shelter had been in and out of prisons, but it was never obvious. The only difference between being free and imprisoned is a bad choice or two. Tracy asked Tory how Harry happened to find Amanda.

"Well, when he got out of prison he met Amanda's mother, and they got married. Then he got arrested again and he went back to prison. Amanda's mom left and he never heard from her again. He didn't even know she had a baby! But he's been on his own and working for a long time now, so he looked for Amanda's mom and found her and *then* found out about his daughter! Wow, doesn't that sound like a movie or something? For a long time when he called, Amanda's mom kept telling him to leave them alone. But finally she talked to him. He told her he has settled down and even bought the bakery. I think he still loves her, Mom."

"You mean Amanda's mom?" Tracy knew exactly what Tory meant, but she was getting such a kick out of Tory's enthusiasm.

"Yes. He didn't even know Amanda was born until she finally told him. Wow, he was shocked to find out he was a dad! Anyway, they've been talking a lot on the phone, and then Amanda and her mom drove up here yesterday. I asked Harry if he almost freaked out, and he said, 'Yes!' Wow, he acts so happy."

Tracy suddenly thought about Paul and how happy she would feel if he called her on the phone at that very moment. Then she realized this was her first thought of Paul all day.

"What is Amanda's mother's name?" Tracy asked, trying to shake the nagging sadness.

"I think he calls her Sue Ann. He's going to take them both out for dinner tonight. I'll bet he's about to freak out about that, too."

Tracy glanced into the rearview mirror and saw Tory looking jubilant; Kathleen had fallen asleep. Tracy felt a welcome peace come over her. She thought, *There is so much good in the world if we just remember to recognize it. There are positive things happening all around us if we will just see them.* For the first time in many weeks Tracy felt her heart was light again.

She felt like herself! And even if it didn't last for long, that was all right. It would come back. And maybe next time it will last for days, and the time after that, perhaps weeks.

Tracy knew that if she and the children had stayed at home feeling miserable, she wouldn't be feeling this way now. She thought about what she had so often told others: *When we fill someone's bucket, we fill our own at the same time.* They had filled the buckets of many homeless people by helping to pre-pare food for them and cleaning up afterward. They had also filled the buckets of the men who worked at the shelter by working, talking and laughing with them. Tracy felt good about that, and so did Tory, Cody and Kathleen. It did fill their buckets. The plan had worked extremely well. But there was a surprise element that would have never entered Tracy's mind: *The homeless men filled their buckets more than Tracy's family had filled theirs.* By sharing their experiences openly and hon-estly, the homeless men taught them valuable things that no one else could have taught them. For instance, they taught about judgment. Tracy knew she would never drive by a park or homeless shelter again and have thoughts like "what did they do to deserve that lifestyle?" or "why don't they just get a job?" These humble, troubled people gave a family in crisis an education that can't be given in school, in the workplace or at home. They filled the family's buckets so uniquely.

Tracy knew now that the children and she would survive; they would be happy again. Circumstances and other people are not in charge of whether our buckets are full or empty; we are. Understanding that truth gave Tracy such comfort that she slept all the way through the night for the first time in many weeks.

	LET'S TALK ABOUT IT
1	What feeling or feelings did Tracy have when her husband left?
2	What feeling or feelings did each of the children have when they learned that their father had left? (Tory, Cody, and Kathleen)
3	Before their first day of working at the homeless shelter, how do you think Tracy felt about going there?
4	Why do you think Tracy, Tory, Cody, and Kathleen felt better after doing their volunteer work?
5	Is anything in your own life similar to the challenge of Tracy's family?
6	What are the things you learned from this true story?

CHAPTER 2

Mr. Archer

Bucketfillers Can Come into Our
Lives in Surprising Ways

Ellen Farrell, an elementary school principal, moved to a new neighborhood. She had lived out in the country on 10 acres for many years. She was ready for a change. The new house was smaller—just perfect for her and 10-year-old Spud, a cocker spaniel and Ellen's best friend since he was a pup. The yard was also small, and the grass would be quick and easy to cut. Sunshine blanketed the front yard, and there was lots of room for flowers. In the back were tall, mature shade trees.

Ellen stood at the kitchen sink and looked out the window at Spud in the backyard. He was barking at butterflies and squirrels. Ellen sighed. *He's getting old,* she thought. *No chasing anymore, just barking.* Ellen was concerned that even though Spud moved slowly these days, he may still wander out of their yard and bother the neighbors. After all, he was used to lots of space with no restrictions.

In less than a week, Ellen's worry was confirmed; she found herself yelling, "SPUD! Come home, Spud!" several times a day. He would obediently come home, limping through the hedge from the neighbor's yard. *Uh-oh,* worried Ellen. *He's going into Mr. Archer's yard. I hope Mr. Archer likes dogs.*

Ellen was welcomed by a few of the people on her street, but she had not yet met Mr. Archer. He obviously kept to himself.

"He's an elderly man who doesn't talk to people," a neighbor told her. "Ever since his wife died, he's been reclusive and unfriendly."

School started right after Labor Day, and Ellen was busy. Every afternoon when she came home, Ellen turned on the front sprinklers, watered the flowers and let Spud out into the backyard. One day as she walked out onto the patio to relax, something caught her eye. *What's that?* she thought when she noticed a tall, brown paper bag on a corner of the cement. Ellen carefully walked close enough to peer into the bag. *OH, NO!* The bag contained more dog poop than she had ever seen before in one place. The smell was awful! There was a bright, yellow note stuck to the top of the bag. It read, "OBVIOUSLY THIS IS YOURS! KEEP THAT MUTT IN HIS OWN YARD!"

"Oh, Spud," she said to the dog. "We're in trouble with Mr. Archer. I better keep a much closer eye on you." Spud looked at Ellen and tilted his head as if to say, "Huh?" Ellen wrinkled her nose, held her arm straight out in front of her and picked up the sack. It was heavy, and the bottom fell out of the bag, spilling the contents onto the patio. *Yuck,* thought Ellen. *Mr. Archer must have been collecting this for a long time.*

As Ellen looked at the mess, she felt irritation bubble up inside of her. This would not be fun to clean up. *Mr. Archer could have just come over and told me Spud had been in his yard,* Ellen thought. *This is not a good way to settle a problem! I know some people who would just throw that poop right back into his yard!*

At that moment, a memory from long ago came to Ellen's mind. When she was seven years old, a neighbor backed out of his driveway and hit Ellen's dad's car. She saw it happen from her bedroom window. The neighbor, Mr. Redmond, got out of his car and inspected the damage. He looked nervously at his watch, then got out a piece of paper and scribbled a note. He stuck it under the windshield wiper of her dad's car, got back into his own car and drove away.

Just before supper, Ellen's dad discovered the badly dented driver's door. He read the note: "I'm sorry I did this. I will pay whatever it costs. *Jim Redmond.*"

"What kind of a man just writes a note about causing so much damage!" raged Ellen's father. "He should have come to our door and spoken with me personally! When he gets home I'll go over there and give him a piece of my mind. What a jerk!" he shouted to Ellen's mother. His yelling frightened Ellen. She wished that Mr. Redmond hadn't driven away in such a hurry.

The next morning was Saturday. At 8:00 Ellen's father walked across the street to Mr. Redmond's house and pounded on his door. He was calmer by then, but still very angry. Ellen watched again from her window. Mr. Redmond opened the door. Ellen's dad leaned in toward Mr. Redmond, and Ellen could hear his loud voice. He pointed his finger at Mr. Redmond and got even louder. When he was finished, Mr. Redmond said something. Her dad became very still, turned around and walked back toward their house. Mr. Redmond shut his door.

When her dad came into the house, her mother asked what Mr. Redmond had said. Ellen knew that her mom felt bad when her husband lost his temper.

"Well, he said he'll pay for the damage and that he was sorry.

I asked why he didn't have the guts to come over and tell me to my face what he had done. He said the nursing home had just called and that his mom was really bad. They told him to hurry. She died a few minutes after he got there."

Ellen noticed her dad's voice was very low. He had a bad temper sometimes, but now Ellen could tell he felt sorry.

A few years later when Ellen and her father were having a talk, he told her that he had learned a painful lesson that day. "Ellen, honey," he said, "always give people a chance before you judge them. In fact, don't judge them at all. You just never know what they are going through. I lost my temper and wound up sounding and feeling like a fool. Mr. Redmond was going through a rough time, and I made it worse. He could have gotten angry with me, but he didn't."

Ellen looked at the mess on the corner of the patio. She turned around and walked through the hedge to Mr. Archer's back door. *I'll introduce myself and apologize,* she thought. Ellen knocked on his door and waited. No answer. She rang the doorbell several times. Still no answer. *I know he's home,* she mumbled to herself. *I saw his car in the driveway.* After a few minutes, Ellen went back home.

Autumn came, and the leaves turned to golds and reds. Ellen had still not even caught a glimpse of Mr. Archer. And despite repeated efforts, she could not get him to answer his door.

One cool Sunday morning after a wind storm, Ellen was picking up branches in her backyard. Some of them were quite large. *Must have been quite a storm,* thought Ellen. She straightened up and rubbed her back. As she did, Ellen looked over the hedge into Mr. Archer's yard. His lawn was littered with branches, just like hers. She smiled. After she dumped her armload of branches into the garbage can, Ellen went into

Mr. Archer's yard and began to pick up twigs and branches. An hour later, the yard was cleared and a big pile of branches lay near the hedge. She went home to get some trash bags.

That night as Ellen drifted off to sleep, she thought of the stinky surprise that Mr. Archer had left on her patio two months ago, and she giggled. She wondered if he looked out a window at her as she picked up the sticks in his yard. If he did, what was he thinking?

It was a windy, stormy autumn, and Ellen picked up the branches in Mr. Archer's yard several times. She had still never seen him. *When does he shop for groceries? In the middle of the night?* she wondered. There were never other cars in his driveway. *Gosh, no visitors.* Ellen was sure by then that Mr. Archer had cut himself off from everyone.

On the Wednesday before Thanksgiving, Ellen worked late at the school. By the time she pulled into her driveway, it was dark outside. She was tired and hungry. As she fished around in her purse for her keys, Ellen caught sight of something at the front door. It was difficult to make out what it was, so she shined her little flashlight at it. There was a familiar-looking brown bag with a bright, yellow note stuck near the top. *Not this again! Oh, Spud, I thought for sure you were staying in our yard,* Ellen moaned. She approached the bag slowly, holding her breath. She shined the light on the note. It read, "HEAT THIS UP." Ellen was shocked. *Heat it up? Oh my, he must **really** be angry this time!*

Knowing better than to try to pick it up, Ellen touched the bag with the side of her foot. She tried to scoot it aside, but she felt something hard. She cautiously shined the light into the bag. *Aluminum foil?* Ellen could no longer hold her breath. She exhaled loudly and then sniffed. *Hmmmmm . . . Beef stew?*

Soup? Sure smells good! As she picked up the bag, Ellen looked at Mr. Archer's house. A living room curtain that had been pulled aside quickly fell back into place.

Ellen felt good inside as she heated up the homemade vegetable beef soup. A feeling of happiness flooded over her. She ate the delicious soup and thought of her father. And she was very grateful that she hadn't thrown Spud's poop back into Mr. Archer's yard.

During the following three years, Ellen and Mr. Archer became friends. He finally answered the door when she knocked to thank him for the soup and to return his bowl. They often talked, but never for long. Mr. Archer still stayed inside the house most of the time. One time when Ellen waited for him to open his door and he didn't answer, she peered through the nearby window to see if he was all right. She saw him sitting at the kitchen table looking at a photo album. She almost rapped on the window, but then changed her mind and went home.

Ellen continued to pick up the branches in his yard. She even raked his leaves as he grew older and feebler. She took his garbage can to the end of his driveway on Mondays. She brought his mail to the front door from the box at the street and even did some grocery shopping for him. In return, and when she least expected it, Ellen would come home from school and find a familiar-looking paper bag at the front door with a bright, yellow note stuck to it. Sometimes there was a loaf of home-baked bread inside, a small pitcher of freshly squeezed juice, or a bowl of soup. Now when Ellen looked over at Mr. Archer's house, more often than not she would see him at the window, and he would give her a smile and a wave.

One late summer Sunday, Spud died. As Ellen gently placed her beloved friend's blanket-wrapped body in a hole under the maple tree, Mr. Archer stood next to her.

"Spud always barked at the squirrel that taunted him from this tree," Ellen said quietly.

"Yes, I know," said Mr. Archer. He put his arm around her tightly as she cried.

Two years later, Mr. Archer became very ill. An ambulance took him to the hospital, and Ellen followed it in her car. When he got settled in a room, she stood next to his bed. He had tubes going into his nose, and his breathing was shallow. He was weak and could barely hold his eyes open. Machines were beeping. Ellen knew in her heart then that he wouldn't be coming home, but strangely, that seemed all right. She covered his chilly hand with her warm one, and he blinked.

He smiled up at her and asked in a whisper, "You remember that bag of dog doo-doo I left on your patio some years back?"

"Oh, yes, I do recall that," Ellen grinned.

"Well, that wasn't very nice. I've been meaning to say I'm sorry for that."

"No problem, Mr. Archer. I'm sorry Spud was using your yard instead of mine."

"How come you didn't get mad? I was mad. And I thought we'd have ourselves a nice war going. You know, just keep throwing the doo-doo back and forth. Might have been fun." Mr. Archer gave her a little smile.

"I almost got angry. But I thought of my dad, and I just chose not to. Even though you and I got off to a bad start, it was better to become friends, don't you think?" Ellen asked.

"Yes. A bad start," he mumbled softly. Ellen could see he was very sleepy; his eyes were closing again. "But it sure is a good finish."

"Yes, for sure. It's a great finish." And Ellen sat down next to Mr. Archer's bed and stayed with him for a while as he slept.

	LET'S TALK ABOUT IT
1	What feelings do you think Mr. Archer had before Ellen and Spud moved next door? What had happened in his life?
2	Do you think that Mr. Archer was happy that Ellen and Spud moved next door to him?
3	How do you think Ellen felt when Mr. Archer left the bag of dog poop on her patio?
4	Who taught Ellen a valuable lesson when she was a child, and how did she use that lesson in this situation?
5	Name the bucketfillers and bucketdippers in this story. Was anyone both?
6	Is anything in your own life similar to this true story?

CHAPTER 3

Francine

Our Buckets Can Be Filled
at the Perfect Time

The telephone rang. *Who would be calling at this hour?* Francine asked herself. "Hello?"

"Francine, this is Father Joseph," said the caller.

"Oh, hi there, Father Joseph. Is something wrong?"

"No, not really. Are you still coming to midnight mass tonight?" he asked.

"Yes, but we're running a bit late. The kids are getting dressed. What's up?"

"Well, there's a new family, the Thompsons; they just arrived at church. Mrs. Thompson looked worried, so I asked what was going on. It seems their car ran out of gas just as they pulled into the parking lot. Do you have a gas can?"

"I think so." Francine thought about it. *Yes, it's red.* She could picture it on a shelf in the garage. "Yes, we do! Want me to get it filled and bring it with us?"

"Oh, yes, Francine, that would be wonderful. I would appreciate it, and so will they. There are three children, all quite young. It's their first time here at St. Mary's. They feel embarrassed not having money with them. I think they're wishing they had stayed home tonight," Father Joseph said.

"Do they have to drive far? I don't think our gas can holds very much," asked Francine.

"No, no. They're just new to the area and got a bit lost finding the church. A gallon will get them home for Christmas," he replied.

"Okay, Father, no problem. Be there ASAP!"

"Bless you, Francine, and your children. May God watch over you as you drive tonight," said Father Joseph. And he hung up.

Francine threw her coat on. "KIDS!" she shouted up the stairs. "Come on, let's go! We have an important stop to make on the way to church!"

"Coming!" they both yelled.

The two children climbed into the back seat of the car as Francine grabbed the dusty gas can.

"Mom, what's that can for?" asked six-year-old Mason.

"We're going to fill a bucket tonight, honey. You'll see," answered Francine as she backed out of the garage. Light snow was just beginning to fall.

"Hurray! Maybe we'll have a white Christmas, Mom!" shouted Mason.

"Mason, stop shouting! You're breaking my eardrums," snapped Kathryn, Mason's 12-year-old sister.

Francine focused on the road and tried to think of a gas station that might be open at this hour on Christmas Eve. *Gosh, I didn't think of that. It's late on a holiday.* She turned in a direction that led away from St. Mary's.

"Uh, Mom, you're going the wrong direction," said Kathryn. "Where are we going?"

"A family at church needs gas for their car, and Father Joseph asked us to get some so they can get home tonight. I'm hoping that Herman's will be open. If it's closed, I'm not sure what we'll do." Francine was starting to feel worried.

"Is this like a favor? Are we doing something nice and bucketfilling?" asked Mason.

"Yes, absolutely," answered Francine. She smiled at her son in the rearview mirror.

"Oh, cool. We're being bucketfillers on Christmas Eve. I hope that Santa Claus can see this!" Mason shouted in the direction of his window.

Kathryn rolled her eyes and sighed. "Mason, when we do something nice it's not because we want an extra present from Santa. You're such a dork."

"Hey! That's bucketdipping! Mom, Kathryn called me a name. She's a bucketdipper on Christmas!" Mason complained.

"Oh, for heaven's sakes, you two. Just look out the window and see if you can spot Santa out there. He should be in our area about now."

Kathryn rolled her eyes. Mason leaned over to her and whispered, "I hope you get rotten stuff in your Christmas stocking!"

"I heard that!" warned Francine.

It was snowing harder. The flakes were swirling around in the glow of the streetlights. Francine loved to watch the snow, but right now she was focused on looking for the lights at Herman's. She turned the corner, and saw the lights were on! She pulled up next to a gas pump, and as she opened her door the station lights went off. It was exactly midnight.

Oh, no! He's closing up! thought Francine. She grabbed the gas can, jumped out of the car and went to the door. She rapped loudly on the glass. "Hello? Hello?" A man appeared on the other side of the door. He turned the "Open" sign over so that it read "Closed" and pointed to the sign. Francine pointed to the gas can and started jumping up and down in desperation.

Oh, Mom! How embarrassing, thought Kathryn. *This is going to be the most humiliating Christmas in history.* She slouched down in her seat.

The man shook his head *no* and kept pointing to the sign. Francine put the gas can down on the pavement and put the palms of her hands together in a praying motion. She said, "Come on, please. Just one gallon."

"Wow, that guy is such a bucketdipper. Look at Mom. Doesn't he care that it's Christmas?" said Mason.

Kathryn rolled her eyes and said, "Mason, be quiet. Give the guy a break. Maybe he's from Asia or Sweden or someplace and doesn't even know it's Christmas."

The man's expression finally softened a bit, and he partially opened the door.

"Just a gallon?" he asked.

"Yes, just a gallon! It's for a family at church." Francine smiled at the man.

"Well, okay, go ahead. I haven't shut off the pumps yet," he said.

"Thank you!" said Francine. Before she turned back to the gas pump, Francine reached into her coat pocket and pulled out two dollar bills. "Here, thank you," she said as she held them out for the man.

He put up his hand and said, "No, no. Just get your gas. I locked up the cash register already."

"Well, if you're sure about that, thank you so much. And Merry Christmas!" As Francine turned toward the gas pump, she smiled at her children.and excitedly waved the dollar bills at them.

"Look! He's a bucketfiller!" exclaimed Mason. Kathryn smiled, but just a little.

Francine put the filled gas can in the trunk and sniffed her hands. "Whew!" she said as she got back into the car. "I must have spilled some. Now my hands smell like gas."

"Yuck, Mom. I can smell it back here. Guess who I'm *not* sitting with in church?" asked Kathryn.

"Oh, good, you're not sitting with us," Mason commented.

"Little bucketdipper!" Kathryn hissed at her brother.

Francine turned back toward the church and glanced at the clock. It was already several minutes past midnight; mass had started. She pushed the accelerator and looked in her side mirrors to see if any cars were around. She saw no one, so she accelerated a bit more, looking nervously from the clock to the speedometer and back to the clock. Just as she was passing the darkened parking lot of a grocery store, she noticed the police car. The headlights were off, but she could see the officer sitting at the wheel. *Uh-oh*, she thought. He pulled out of the parking lot behind her. The red and blue light on top of his car started flashing. Francine, Kathryn and Mason heard the BWOOP BWOOP of the siren signaling Francine to pull over.

"Oh, no!" Francine and Kathryn groaned in unison.

"COOL!" exclaimed Mason.

Francine slowly steered the car to the curb and stopped. The police car stopped behind her, the car's lights flashing brightly, alternately coloring the falling snow red and blue. She saw the officer open his car door. Francine rolled her window down and waited for him.

"In a hurry tonight?" he asked as he leaned down and looked into the car.

"Hi!" said Mason.

"Mason, be quiet!" whispered Kathryn.

"Yes, Officer, I'm so sorry. I am in a bit of a hurry. How fast was I going?"

"I clocked you going 48 miles per hour in a 35 zone. And the roads are getting slick. May I see your license, registration and proof of insurance, please, ma'am?" The police officer peered into the back seat. Mason was grinning from ear to ear, and Kathryn looked out the window closest to her as if something more interesting was catching her attention. *This is just perfect*, she thought. *Getting a ticket on Christmas Eve, and Mason will tell everyone. Just great. I can hear people laughing already.*

"The man at Herman's just filled our buckets!" exclaimed Mason to the officer.

"Filled your what?" asked the officer.

"Our buckets! He gave Mom some free gas!" Mason explained proudly.

The policeman looked at Francine with a puzzled look on his face. "What is he talking about, ma'am?" he asked her. Kathryn groaned and covered her face with her hands.

Francine looked nervously at the clock. They would be even later now, and she hadn't had a ticket in over 20 years. So she spoke very fast. "Well, sir, Father Joseph called us and asked us to bring gas for some people at church who got lost and ran out of gas on the way to church. So we did that, but the station was closing when we got to Herman's which was the only station I thought might be open. The man had just locked the door and turned the sign over to read *Closed,* but I pleaded for him to open up for just a minute so we could fill the gas can for the people who needed it." Francine was out of breath. "And so he did," she added.

"Yes, ma'am, that's nice. But what did your son mean about filling buckets? I thought you filled a gas can." *Oh, no,* thought Kathryn, *here she goes again.* When her mother got nervous, she talked too much and too quickly. It was very embarrassing.

"Oh, well, you see, officer, we all have invisible buckets, and you have one, too, and when people are nice to us they fill our buckets, and we call them bucketfillers. But when people are not nice to us, they dip in our buckets and they are bucket-dippers, so Mason means the man at the gas station filled our buckets by letting us fill the gas can," Francine said, taking a big breath at the end of her long, fast speech.

"Hmmm . . . Interesting. I never heard of that before," said the officer. "Please wait here for a moment."

The police officer took Francine's drivers license and went back to his car. Francine watched him, thinking, *Oh, please hurry, please hurry, and please don't give me a ticket!*

"What's he doing, Mom? Is he going to take you to jail? Can we go with you? Will Santa Claus find us if we go to jail?" asked Mason, who was starting to feel worried. Kathryn felt too humiliated to speak.

"No, Mason, moms and children do not go to jail," Francine assured her son. She watched the officer as he walked back to their car.

"Well, ma'am, it looks like you have a clean record. No tickets," he said, again leaning down to her window.

"Yes, sir, I do try to be a careful driver," answered Francine.

"It seems to me, this being Christmas Eve and all, if I give you a ticket I would be a bucketdipper. Is that true?" the police officer asked, looking at Francine and then back at Mason.

"Yes, you would be dipping in our buckets!" Mason announced. He paused for a moment and then added, "Big time!" Kathryn gasped and slid down lower in her seat.

Francine added, "Well, sir, I would say, yes. Although you would be doing your job, you would definitely be dipping." She smiled at the officer.

"In that case, ma'am, I'll let you off this time with a verbal warning. Since you're being bucketfillers for some folks at church, I'll be a bucketfiller, too. Please slow down, and have a

Merry Christmas." He handed Francine's license back to her, smiled and turned back toward his car.

"Oh, thank you! And Merry Christmas to you, too!" Francine called out her window.

"Wow, that was so cool," said Mason.

"Yes, it certainly was cool," said Francine. She looked at the clock. "And we will arrive at church just in time to get this gas to the people who need it. Wait until Father Joseph hears about all of this! Tonight has become the perfect Christmas Eve."

Yes, just perfect, we'll be the only people totally late for church and Mom will take forever telling everyone why, thought Kathryn, rolling her eyes. But she smiled, just a little.

LET'S TALK ABOUT IT	
1	Who in this story do you believe is a bucketfiller most of the time?
2	Is there anyone in this story you believe is often a bucketdipper?
3	What choice did Ellen make at the gas station that helped her get the needed gas? Could she have chosen to be a bucketdipper at the gas station? If she had, what do you think might have happened?
4	What choice did Ellen make when the police officer pulled her over for speeding? If she had chosen to be a bucketdipper by getting angry, what do you think might have happened?
5	What character in this story do you think learned the biggest lesson about the importance of choosing to be a bucketfiller?
6	Has anything happened in your life that is similar to this true story?

CHAPTER 4

Julia and Mr. H.

We Can Be Bucketfillers for People Who Need Us

Julia stood at the kitchen window and watched her children play in the yard. Their blonde hair blew in the wind as they ran. *Blonde hair, just like mine,* thought Julia. *And just like Mom's.* She smiled. Sometimes Julia wondered if her dad's hair was ever blonde. Now he was bald, but she saw pictures of him when he was newly married to Mom. It was brown and curly then. Maybe it was blonde when he was little. But she knew she would never ask him about that, because she hadn't spoken to her father in over two years.

Julia sometimes wished that her relationship with him was better, but she knew it wouldn't be because he didn't want it that way. It used to hurt a lot, but Julia was now accepting his choice and actually felt all right about it. In fact, she rarely thought of him.

"When I do think about it," Julia said to Sherry, her best friend since childhood, "I know the relationship with Dad was always tough, even when I was little. He was angry almost all of the time. I used to blame myself. I'd think maybe if I was prettier or my grades in school were better, he'd be nicer. Sounds silly now."

Sherry shook her head and said, "I can remember he shouted all the time. We could hear him from my house."

"Yes, that embarrassed me," said Julia softly.

"Well, it wasn't your fault, Jules. I don't know how you lived like that. Or your mom, either. Thank goodness they got divorced!" Sherry frowned just thinking about it.

Julia said, "I thought it was a good thing when they split. But I still wanted him to be good to me. I wanted him to approve of something I did, to appreciate who I am. Even to this day I wish my father would love me—like your dad did. I still miss him so much."

Julia looked away from Sherry as she felt tears coming to her eyes. *Darn it.*

Am I ever going to get past this? And Sherry doesn't need to be reminded of her father's death, she thought.

"I think your dad loves you, Jules. He just doesn't love himself. He doesn't know how to show love to others because he can't stand himself," said Sherry.

"I know, I know. Hey, let's change the subject. Let's chase the kids!"

Julia and Sherry got up from their lawn chairs and yelled, "Here we come!" to their children. The kids screamed and ran in different directions.

"Catch us, Mom!" they all shouted. There was Bailey, nine, her brother Isaac, six, and Sherry's son, Scott, seven.

Bailey and Scott were growing up as best friends just as Julia and Sherry had. Julia often thought of the first time they met thirty years ago. Her family moved into the neighborhood just before Julia's fifth birthday; they were outside unloading the truck when Sherry's family walked over.

"Hi. Welcome to the neighborhood," said Sherry's dad as he held his hand out to Julia's dad. "I'm Phil Haller, this is my wife,

Rhonda, and this little dark-haired girl is our daughter, Sherry."

Julia will always remember looking at Mr. H. that first time. He smiled and gently tapped Sherry on the head as he said her name. Julia could see right away how much he loved her.

"Wanna play?" asked four-year-old Sherry, looking at Julia. Julia was quiet.

"Go ahead," Julia's mother said to her. "Have some fun while we get settled."

"Okay," Julia replied, and off they ran to Sherry's house. From that day forward, they were together almost all the time.

Usually the girls played at Sherry's house because things were happier there. They spent time at Julia's, too, when her dad was at work. When he went hunting for a week in the fall, Sherry would sleep over at Julia's. Julia felt good about that, because she liked having her friend at her house. But when Julia's father was home, Sherry didn't like to be there.

"Come on, Jules," Sherry would say. "Back to my house."

Julia understood. She didn't like to be at home when her dad was there, either. So they played at Sherry's, and often had dinner at Sherry's. Julia went to the store with Sherry and her dad sometimes, too.

Julia felt shy around Mr. H. for a while. She didn't know why, because he was always smiling and nice. Maybe she expected him to change and be angry all of a sudden. But he never did. He got tired from working, and sometimes he asked the girls to quiet down so he could rest. But he asked nicely. When he came home from work, Sherry ran to him and hugged him, and he picked her up and hugged her back.

Julia didn't know how to act when they did that in front of her. She liked seeing it, but it made her a little sad, too. Julia never knew that there were dads like that until she met the Hallers. So she just stood there and waited. One day after

Mr. H. gave Sherry a "hello hug," he reached out to Julia. She felt strange and just stood there. "Well, come on over here, little Blondie. Can't you give me a hug, too?" Julia remembered being very surprised.

"Go on, Jules. Don't be such a baby!" said Sherry as she pushed her friend toward her dad.

Mr. H. picked six-year-old Julia up into his arms and squeezed. She put her arms around his neck and liked how warm his cheek felt against hers. She never forgot that feeling. It was so good to be held like that by a dad. She felt safe—and loved.

Julia thought of that first hug from Mr. H. often through the years. Sometimes she used to wonder why it was such a big deal. As she grew older and became an adult with children of her own, she understood. All children want to be hugged and loved. Julia's mom hugged her a lot, and she knew her mother loved her. But that couldn't make up for the warm hugs she never got from her dad. So that's why throughout her growing-up years, Julia tried to be at Sherry's house when Mr. H. arrived home from work—to get that hug. Even when she became a teenager, Mr. H. put his arm around her and gave her a squeeze, just like he did with Sherry.

"Your dad is so cool," she would often say to Sherry. Sherry agreed most of the time. Once when she was 13 years old, Sherry was angry at her dad for not allowing her to go to a party where there would be older boys.

"No, he's not cool. He's an idiot!" said Sherry.

"Don't ever say that again!" yelled Julia. She ran home and didn't talk to Sherry for two days.

Sixteen years later, on a Tuesday morning around 11 o'clock, Julia heard her phone ring. Bailey was at school, and Isaac was playing in his room.

"Hello?" No one spoke. Julia waited. "Hello?" Then she heard Sherry crying. "Sherry! What's wrong?" Julia was alarmed.

"Jules, Dad's got cancer. Mom just called me and told me the test results," and Sherry broke into loud sobs.

Julia froze with the phone against her ear. Cancer? Mr. H. has cancer? Her mind raced, searching for words to say to Sherry. All she could think of was, "Sherry, I'll be right there." She hung up the phone, grabbed Isaac and drove to Sherry's. In five minutes she walked through the back door and found Sherry sitting at her kitchen table, with her head down on her arms, crying.

"Oh, Sherry, I'm so sorry. I just can't believe it," said Julia softly. She stroked her friend's hair. "He'll be okay, won't he? They'll do an operation or something, and he'll be okay." Julia tried to soothe her friend. But inside, she, too, was terrified. *How could this happen to Mr. H.? He is such a good man. Why him?*

"No, there's no operation. It's bone cancer," replied Sherry, lifting her head. Her eyes were swollen from crying.

The following days and months were filled with treatments with powerful drugs. Mr. H. also had something called a stem cell transplant. The procedure was dangerous and made Mr. H. very ill; Julia went to the Hallers' every day for a couple of months to take care of him as he regained his strength. After that, there were long periods of time when Mr. H. felt good. He went to work as often as he could, kept smiling and acted normally. But Julia never completely forgot what the doctors had said. This cancer was not curable. Mr. H. would eventually die from it. Julia tried not to think about it. For almost 30 years, Mr. H. had become the father that Julia always wished her own father could be.

Once in a while Mr. H. would smile and say to her, "Jules, you're a grown woman now. Why won't you call me 'Phil'?"

Julia smiled back and said, "Because to me, you're not 'Phil,' that's why. You're 'Mr. H.'" Then he would sigh, shrug his shoulders and say, "Okay, okay."

One day Sherry called on the phone. "Jules, the cancer, it's back. Dad has a fever and he's really sick. Mom just took him to the hospital."

When Mrs. Haller came home from the hospital that night, Mr. H. did not come home with her. She called Julia.

"Honey, will you come over in the morning at 10 o'clock? We're having a family meeting."

Julia assured her she would be there. She didn't sleep well that night. All she could think about was Mr. H. and how warm his cheek felt against hers so many years ago.

The meeting was short. The cancer was back. Mr. H. would be in the hospital for a couple days until they got him stronger, then he'd be home. He would be weak and not able to take care of himself.

"What about another stem cell transplant?" asked Julia. "Why won't they do that?"

"They don't think they could get enough stem cells from him. He's too sick." Mrs. Haller cried then, and Sherry put her arm around her mom.

At the meeting, the Hallers asked Julia if she would again take care of Mr. H. during the day as she had done off and on during the past year. Mrs. Haller needed to work to keep the health insurance, and Sherry and her brothers had to keep the business going that Mr. H. had started many years ago.

Julia agreed to come over every day. She made arrangements with Ryan, her wonderful husband, to be home in time to get Bailey off the school bus. Julia's mother cared for Isaac as often as she could. Everyone pitched in.

When Mr. H. came home from the hospital, Julia was shocked

at how thin he had become in such a short time. He looked very old. But she kept a smile on her face and said, "Okay, Mr. H. You may not like this, but I'm here to make sure you behave yourself. You need to eat to keep up your strength. Mrs. Haller says you're being stubborn about that."

"Oh, no," Mr. H. pretended to groan. "Am I going to have to put up with Jules' nagging?" But he smiled.

Julia helped him get to the sofa.

During the following months, Mr. H. had almost-good days and bad days. Some mornings when Julia got to their house, he was lying on the sofa and staring at the ceiling. He was getting thinner. He didn't want to eat.

"Now look, Mr. H., you need to eat something. What do you feel like having?" Julia acted and sounded stern, but inside she felt like crying. How had this strong man who easily swept her up into his arms when she was a child gotten so weak?

"I can only think of one thing that sounds good. And we don't have it," he answered, sounding tired and grouchy.

"What's that?" asked Julia.

"One of those cinnamon raisin bagels, lightly toasted, with strawberry swirl cream cheese," said Mr. H.

"You mean from Frank's Bagel Shop?" asked Julia with a smile. She knew perfectly well what he meant.

"Yes, that's what I mean, Blondie."

"Well, then, stay right there on the sofa. Don't move. I'll be back in 10 minutes!" Julia was happy to drive a few miles to get something Mr. H. would eat. She had driven with him to Frank's many times in the recent past. But now he was too sick to get into the car.

When she gave him the bagel, he took a few bites.

"Thanks," he said, putting it back on the plate. "I thought I was hungry, but I guess I'm not."

Julia helped him walk down the hall into his home office so they could pay the bills. Mrs. Haller would have done it, but Mr. H. insisted on doing as much as he possibly could.

A few days later, after taking some new medication, he got stronger again. Julia always felt happy when that happened. Sometimes he felt better for an entire week. They would take rides in the car so he could feel the warm spring air on his face. They went to Frank's, and Mr. H. would eat a whole bagel. She drove him to his business so he could check on things and say hello to the employees. Julia could tell that the employees tried not to look shocked when they saw him. He looked so small and much older than his real age. They smiled and shook his hand. Everyone loved Mr. H.

On a Thursday during a doctor's appointment, Mr. H. said to the doctor, "I want to take my family on that trip to Texas. We planned it last year, and I want us to go."

Julia was surprised, but she said nothing. The doctor spoke.

"Phil, I think that's a great idea. You know there isn't much time left for trips, so now is the time to go." The doctor looked right into Mr. H's eyes. "You should leave soon, Phil."

So Mr. H. told his family they were going to Texas. He bought plane tickets and made reservations at a nice hotel. He would take Rhonda, Sherry and Scott, and Sherry's brothers. Julia volunteered to take Sherry's place at work so she could go without worry about the office. The day before they left, Julia took Mr. H. for a transfusion that might keep him strong enough for the week. They talked during the procedure.

"You know, Jules, I appreciate how much you've helped out through all of this."

"No problem. I'm happy to do it." She answered with a smile, but she thought, *I hope he doesn't talk about the cancer. I just don't want him to talk about the cancer.*

"I feel very comfortable with you. I always have, Jules. You're like a daughter. Just like a daughter." Julia thought she might cry. She wanted to tell him that he was just like a father to her. In fact, for many years she had wished he could be her father. He did and said the things a father should do. But at that moment, Julia said nothing. She just smiled.

The next day, the Haller family left for Texas. Julia went to the Hallers' business every day and kept up on Sherry's work. Mr. H. called several times and said they were having a good time. When Julia asked him how he felt, he simply said, "Fine, just fine." The day before the Hallers were scheduled to come home, Sherry called. "We're coming home early. Dad is running a fever. It might just be a cold or the flu, but we're coming back, just in case." Julia hung up the phone. A scared feeling rose up through her body. *Come on, Mr. H. Let's hope it's a cold.*

It wasn't a cold. Mr. H. went straight from the airport to the hospital. The cancer was back, and this time there was nothing the doctors could do to help him get better. Julia went to the hospital and spent every minute with the Hallers. She sat next to Mr. H.'s bed and held his hand. One time she stayed awake all night just watching him so that Mrs. Haller, Sherry and her brothers could sleep.

Mr. H. was very weak, and the doctor said it wouldn't be long before he died. Perhaps it would only be a day or two. When Julia heard those words, they hurt more than anything she could imagine. She had known; they all had known for years that Mr. H. could not beat this cancer. It just felt good to pretend sometimes that he could.

She heard his words from nine days ago in her head. *You're like a daughter. Just like a daughter.* He was right. They had a special bond. Julia knew she was lucky to have this relationship with him. He turned his head slowly toward her, opened his eyes and looked at her. He blinked two times, obviously a signal to her. In her heart, Julia knew what he meant.

"Mr. H., do you want to go home? Do you want to be in your own house now?" Julia asked him. He nodded slightly, *yes*. Julia went into the hall to tell Sherry and Mrs. Haller. They told the doctor, and within an hour an ambulance came to take Mr. H. home. Mrs. Haller and Sherry followed the ambulance in their car, and Julia followed them.

For the first time in a long time, Julia allowed herself to cry. She cried hard. *Get it all out now,* she thought. *Do it now so you can be strong when we get to their house.*

The paramedics brought Mr. H. into the house. There was a hospital bed in the living room waiting for him. They helped settle him in the bed and left.

A hospice nurse arrived and showed Julia how to give Mr. H. the pain medication that would keep him comfortable. She explained after examining Mr. H. that his time would be very short now. Julia inhaled deeply and said, "Okay, thank you." The nurse left, saying she would be back in a couple of hours to check on him.

Sherry, her brothers and Mrs. Haller were talking about something in the kitchen. Julia was alone with Mr. H. She could barely hear his breathing. She held his bony hand.

"Mr. H., I think you can hear me. I want to tell you something." Julia took a deep breath. "You know that day about a week ago when you said I am like a daughter to you?" Julia looked at his face. His eyes were closed; he looked very peaceful.

"I wanted to say something back to you, but I didn't. I wish I had said it then." Julia swallowed hard and did her best to speak clearly so he would understand her. She leaned in very close to his ear.

"Well, Mr. H. You've been a father to me. You are kind and gentle and calm. Your kids are so lucky to have you for a father. I'm lucky to know you, to see how a father should be. Thank you for that. Thank you." Julia started to cry, but she stopped. *There will be time for that later,* she thought.

"And one more thing. You probably won't remember this, but I do. I think about it a lot. When I was six years old, you picked me up and hugged me for the first time. Your cheek felt really warm. Thanks." Julia sat very still and was quiet. She felt a slight squeeze on her hand. It was very weak, but it was definitely a squeeze. *He heard that, he heard me,* Julia thought with gratitude. Tears dripped down her face to her chin, then fell onto the sheet on Mr. H.'s bed.

Mrs. Haller, the boys and Sherry came in then. They stood near Mr. H.'s head, each touching him. Julia held his hand. His breathing stopped, started again and then stopped. Mr. H. sighed a soft sigh, and then he was quiet.

The following days were busy as the Hallers and Julia planned the funeral. Most of what happened seemed to float by in a haze. There were flowers and tears and hugs from friends and relatives. Then that part was over.

Julia and Sherry celebrated Julia's birthday a few weeks later. They did it quietly this time, eating a cupcake at Julia's kitchen table and enjoying the silence until the school bus would bring their children home.

Julia said, "Life is weird sometimes, isn't it?"

Sherry answered, "Yes, it certainly is."

"I miss your dad so much," Julia said.

"Me, too, Jules," said Sherry.

Then they heard the squeaking of bus brakes, shortly followed by little voices shouting, "MOM!"

LET'S TALK ABOUT IT	
1	Why do you think Julia needed Mr. H. in her life?
2	What feelings do you think Julia had when Mr. H. was kind to her?
3	Was there a bucketdipper in this story?
4	How do you think Julia felt about her own father?
5	Was it easy for Julia to choose to take care of Mr. H.? If yes, why? If no, why?
6	Name all of the bucketfillers in this story.
7	Do you think Julia ever felt happy again after Mr. H. died?
8	Is anything in your life similar to this true story?

CHAPTER 5

Rita

We Can Remember to Fill the Buckets of Those We Love the Most

Rita quickly put the breakfast dishes in the sink and glanced at the clock. It was time to leave for school.

"Bye, honey!" she called to her husband, Bill. She heard nothing. "Bill, I'm leaving!" she called again. Rita heard a mumbled reply from upstairs, but she could not make out what he said. *He's probably shaving,* she thought. *I'll call him during my lunch break and see how he's doing.*

Rita was worried about Bill. They had been married for 24 years, and in all that time she had never known him to be so quiet. He wasn't angry, but he almost never spoke to her. When the boys called from college, Rita would chat with them for quite a while and then offer the phone to Bill. He usually said, "They're probably busy with homework. Tell them I said, 'Hi.'"

Rita knew he missed Ben and Justin, their 19-year-old twins. Bill had had a close relationship with his sons since the day they were born. It just wasn't like him to not jump at an opportunity to talk with them. But Bill had been withdrawing from the family more and more since he lost his job a year ago. Rita thought she had tried everything to reassure him that just because he lost his job, her love for him wouldn't change. It wasn't his fault he got laid off along with 2,000 other auto workers that day. Bill and Rita even knew it was coming, and they talked about it. They thought they were prepared for the day he would be officially unemployed. Rita still had her teaching position; they had saved money faithfully over the years, so they felt confident that financially, things would be fine.

However, Bill loved his job; he was proud of what he had accomplished in 22 years with the same company. He started on the assembly line as a young man and worked his way up to assistant supervisor and then supervisor. Bill worked hard. He was honest, smart and never late for work a day in his life. It didn't seem fair that he would lose his job. But both Rita and Bill knew that life was often not "fair." Things happened, and it was up to them to handle whatever came along. As long as they were together, everything would be all right. They had discussed this often, and the conversation would usually end with a big hug.

When the layoff was official, Bill came home from work that last time and said, "Rita, my lovely wife, let's go out for dinner!"

Rita was thrilled that he was taking the bad news so well, so she grabbed his hand, and off they went to dinner. During dinner, Bill talked about everything he would do around the house. The basement needed more work, he wanted to paint the kitchen which had needed a face-lift for several years, and he even promised Rita a new dishwasher that he would install himself. The best part of all for Rita was when he kissed the back of her hand across the dinner table and said, "Now that I won't be working for a while, perhaps we can spend more time together." The entire evening had been wonderful.

The year had not turned out as planned. During that time, Bill had done only one short project in the basement. The kitchen did not get painted, and Rita was still washing dishes by hand. What happened? Bill was never a lazy person, so Rita knew that was not the problem. Frankly, Rita was not as concerned about the unfinished work around the house as she was about Bill's feelings. He had changed from a cheerful, loving man into someone she did not know.

At dinner, he rarely spoke. Rita and their daughter, Jill, would fall silent, too, sometimes glancing at each other with worried expressions. Bill still went to the basketball games to watch Jill's cheerleading. He adored his daughter and wouldn't have missed a game for the world. He smiled and waved at her from the bleachers, but he didn't jump up and yell when their team scored points. He didn't tell her after the games which cheers were his favorites, and they stopped going out for ice cream after the games. Bill was depressed, and everyone in the family realized it, except Bill.

As Rita drove to school that day, she had an excited feeling that she didn't understand. She had been teaching elementary school for 25 years, and she loved it. This year's fourth-grade class was probably one of the best groups of children she had taught in years. But that didn't account for what she was feeling. What was happening?

All the teachers met in the media center for an early morning meeting. They had these staff meetings several times a year, and last week Rita heard what this one would be about; but she had forgotten. *Whatever,* she thought. Her mind wandered back to Bill.

"Good morning," said the speaker. Rita remembered as soon as the principal introduced the speaker that the staff meeting would be about bucketfilling. Rita understood the concept. She would find out during this meeting what her class would learn. She sipped her coffee and listened. Thirty minutes went by.

"Now you'll have the opportunity to do what your older students will be doing in their workshops," said Darcy, the speaker. She passed out forms to all the teachers. Rita looked at hers. At the top was, "Why I Love and Respect You _____." When Darcy explained that they should each choose one person they loved and respected and write at least 10 reasons why they felt that way, Rita knew immediately who she would choose.

She loved and respected her three children, her parents, her sister, and others. But Rita wrote "Bill" in the blank. The ideas flowed easily as Rita wrote. Tears came to her eyes. Then she suddenly stopped. *This is why I felt so excited this morning!* thought Rita. *This is it! Bill is depressed, and although I've been supportive and patient, he needs to read these things and know how I feel about him. I think he knows these things after all these years together, but perhaps I should have expressed them more often. He needs to know them right now!* Although the form was numbered 1 through 10, Rita had completed 12. She put her pen down on the table as Darcy spoke.

"Your assignment is the same as your students' assignment will be. Please take this home, or wherever you need to go to see the person you chose, and read your list, heart to heart, to him or her. Please don't just hand it to them, *read* it. Look this person in the eyes, and read it. You may experience something more beautiful than you can imagine."

Oh my gosh, thought Rita. *Read it to Bill?* Many excuses rushed into Rita's mind. *Looking at each other as I read these would make Bill too uncomfortable. Bill isn't used to expressing feelings so openly. It would be easier to just let him read this on his own.*

"Some of you, perhaps many of you, may be thinking that it

would be easier to simply let the person read what you wrote. You may feel uncomfortable about reading it directly to them. But I promise that if you will take the risk and do it anyway, you may be the creator of a special experience," Darcy said.

What is she, a mind-reader? thought Rita. As she looked around the room at the other teachers, Rita could tell that many of them were feeling uncomfortable with this assignment. *Well, I have the whole day ahead of me to decide,* thought Rita as she folded the paper and put it into her purse.

Later that day, Darcy came to Rita's classroom to lead a workshop. Rita listened and watched intently, amazed that her nine- and 10-year-old students took part with such enthusiasm. It was obvious they were excited to learn about choice, happiness, and how powerful they are in their own lives. Even Larry and Patrick, who almost never sat still, were focused. Then it was time for the Why I Love and Respect You exercise. Darcy explained to the children what she had explained earlier that day to the staff. All the children wrote. When most were finished, Darcy invited volunteers to share aloud with their classmates what they had written.

Rita thought back to that moment in the teachers' workshop. Only two were willing to share. Rita was not one of them. But as she looked around the classroom, many hands went up. As the students read, Rita couldn't help but shed some tears. She dabbed at her eyes with a tissue and listened. Her heart was touched by their openness and honesty. Morgan wrote to her mother. Josh wrote to his dad, which surprised Rita because she knew Josh seldom saw his dad since his parents were divorced. It warmed her heart.

Darcy asked Josh if it would be easy to read his list to his father.

"No," Josh said. "I'll feel kind of shy about it."

Darcy then said, "Yes, I understand that. Many of us feel uncomfortable expressing feelings of love. But will you choose to do it, anyway?"

Josh thought for a couple of seconds and replied, "Yes. Yes, I will." And he smiled.

Those words stuck with Rita for the remainder of the day: *But will you choose to do it, anyway?* Rita knew she would feel uncomfortable if she read her list to Bill.

Why? she asked herself. *Why should I feel uncomfortable? My husband is my best friend! And perhaps if I read to him all my feelings of love, he'll feel better. He feels so useless since he lost his job. He feels so lost. But he knows I love him. He knows that, doesn't he? I make dinner and wash his clothes; we play chess in the evenings and watch movies. I hold his hand like I've always done. We've been together for so long. He must realize I love him. Doesn't he?*

Rita knew at that exact moment that she would read her list to Bill. Assuming that Bill knows she loves him suddenly wasn't enough. Why hadn't she thought of this before? Just because Rita understood why she loves and respects her husband doesn't mean that he understands it. Bill deserves to be told!

That night Rita made Bill's favorite dinner: meatloaf, mashed potatoes and green beans. While Rita was preparing the food, she thought about how much she missed Bill being in the kitchen. It was their tradition to work together on dinners. Rita always came home from school about an hour before Bill came home from work. He would honk the horn one time as he drove into the garage, come into the house and give her a kiss, and go upstairs to change into comfortable clothes. Then he would come back to the kitchen to help her with the meal. If Rita didn't need help, Bill would sit at the table and ask her about her day, and Rita would ask him about his. Since he lost his job, Rita would come into the house knowing Bill was there, but he would not be around to greet her.

She would shout, "Hi, honey!" Then she would listen for his reply, which usually came from upstairs.

"Up here!" he would answer.

I know he feels awkward about not having a workday to talk about, thought Rita, *but I miss talking to Bill. Doesn't he know that? He should know that. Maybe he felt his success at work was his most important quality. But I don't think that.* She sighed and went about fixing dinner.

Jill came into the kitchen. "Hey, Mom," she said.

"Hey, yourself," Rita answered. "How was school?"

"Fine. I have cheerleading practice after dinner. Are we eating soon?"

"At the regular time. Your dad's favorite."

"Uh-oh. What did you do wrong?" Jill teased. She knew her mom had been making extra efforts for many months to get her dad back to being himself. But nothing seemed to work. Jill was worried, too, but at age 15 didn't have any idea of how she could help him.

"Very funny," said Rita to her daughter. "Would you please set the table?"

When dinner was ready, Rita shouted upstairs, "Bill, dinner's ready!"

"Be right down," was his reply.

As the three of them ate, Jill talked about school and her concerns about the upcoming midterm exams. Rita talked about the bucketfilling workshop that she and her students had experienced that morning. She glanced at Bill as she spoke, but he was looking down at his food. He did say, "Sounds interesting," but Rita could tell he was lost in his own thoughts, as usual.

When they were finished eating and Jill was about to leave the table, Rita put her hand on her daughter's arm. She said, "Honey, just sit here a moment, will you? I have something for your father, and I'd like you to hear it, too." Jill looked startled but stayed seated.

Bill looked at Rita with a concerned expression. Rita got up from the table, went to her purse and pulled out the list she had written that morning. She sat back down and pulled her chair close to Bill.

"Bill, I have something I want to read to you," said Rita. *Oh my gosh, this is going to be hard,* she thought. *What if I cry? Oh, it doesn't matter if I cry. I just hope this will help to pull Bill out of his depression.* Rita took a deep breath and looked at her husband's face before she started to read. He was looking directly at her, but his expression had returned to its usual "neutral."

Come on, Bill. Show some enthusiasm. Where's my best friend? Is he still in there somewhere? thought Rita. She cleared her throat nervously and began to read.

Why I Love and Respect You, Bill:

- You've been the best husband a woman could wish for.
- You are loyal.
- You are trustworthy, honest and always keep your word.
- You are the hardest worker I've ever known.

Rita looked up at Bill as she read. He sat there, expressionless. He had stopped looking at her and was staring down at the table. *Can't he hear me?* wondered Rita. *Why isn't he smiling?*

- I would rather talk with you than anyone else.
- You are a wonderful, loving father to our three children.
- You are the favorite dad of all of our children's friends.

Bill didn't move, nor did he look at Rita. *Come on, Bill, please. Show some reaction!* Rita was feeling disappointed and worried, but she kept reading.

- You give the best back rubs.
- You are the most handsome husband I've ever had.

Rita was hoping for a laugh from Bill with that one. It was a little joke they had between them. Rita had been married only once, and that was to Bill. He showed no reaction.

Bill, please, Rita pleaded silently. *I should have told you these things a long time ago, but please don't let it be too late for them to touch your heart!*

- You go to garage sales with me even though you don't enjoy them; you tell me you go to watch my face when I get excited over finding something we really don't need. I feel good about that because I know it means you love me.
- I cannot picture living even one day without you in it.
- You are my first and only love.

That was the entire list. Rita took a breath and looked at Bill. He was still sitting motionless, staring down at the table.

"Wow, Mom, that was cool," said Jill. She shifted nervously in her chair and looked at her dad. "If you'll excuse me, I'm going upstairs to change my clothes for practice." She left the table and quickly ran upstairs.

Rita and Bill sat alone at the kitchen table. Rita was trying to control her frustration. She felt terribly let down by Bill's lack of reaction to her heartfelt expressions of love.

"Bill . . . ," she began.

Her husband put his finger to his lips, motioning her to be still. Without looking at her, he stood up. He took the one step toward her that separated them. Bill reached down to Rita's hands, took them in his, and pulled her gently to a standing position. He then put his arms around his wife, buried his face in her neck and began to cry. Rita hugged her husband tightly, and when she did that, he sobbed. His whole body shook, and his tears dripped down Rita's neck.

Oh, Bill, she thought. *Oh, Bill.* Rita was surprised at his strong show of emotion. Bill had only cried once before during their marriage, and that was when Rita's mother died. But it was nothing like this.

When his crying slowed and Bill could speak, he lifted his head and looked into his wife's eyes. His face was wet with tears.

"Rita, you'll never know how much I needed to hear those things." He began to cry again, more softly this time. He sniffed and wiped his nose on his sleeve, like the boys did when they were little. "I've been such a selfish, sulking fool over this job loss. Can you and the kids ever forgive me?"

Rita looked long and hard into the face of the man she thought had been lost. He was still there! She felt an over-whelming sense of relief and gratitude.

"There is nothing to forgive, sweetheart. Nothing at all." They stood in the kitchen, holding on to each other for a long time.

	LET'S TALK ABOUT IT
1	What were the feelings that Rita was having about her husband, Bill?
2	What were Bill's feelings after he lost his job, and why do you think he felt that way?
3	How was Rita feeling as she read her list to Bill? Why did she feel that way?
4	Why do you think Bill first showed no reaction when the list was read to him? How was he was feeling?
5	Name all the feelings you think that Rita and Bill had after she finished reading her list.
6	Do you think it was important for Rita to fill Bill's bucket? If yes, why?

CHAPTER 6

Luke

Family Members Can
Be Great Bucketfillers

Nine-year-old Luke got up early for school, as usual. It took him longer to get ready for school because he moved so slowly, especially in the morning. Juvenile arthritis was something he had been dealing with since he could remember. His joints hurt, sometimes a lot. But most of all, it hurt when the kids at school didn't invite him to play at recess. Luke spent every recess alone, and he ate lunch alone, too. Yes, he walked differently, but he felt the same inside as everyone else, didn't he? He wondered about that many times. Luke had become very quiet, and he kept to himself. And he almost never smiled.

"Morning, Luke!" Marcus greeted his younger brother. "Want some cereal?"

Now Luke smiled. "Sure," he replied. Luke adored Marcus. He thought he was the best 16-year-old brother a boy could have. Even though Marcus was a popular athlete in high school with lots of friends, Marcus always had time for Luke. He even invited him to shoot baskets with the guys when his buddies came over. The only times Luke could remember that Marcus got angry with him was when Luke felt sorry for himself about the arthritis. "Just knock it off, Luke. You're gonna outgrow it!" Marcus would snap.

"Mom went to work early again. So eat something, will ya'?" Marcus smiled again.

They both crunched on cereal. "Hey, you're coming to the game tonight, right?" Marcus asked.

"Yes!" Luke said with his mouth full, dripping milk back into the bowl. Going to his brother's basketball games was his favorite thing to do.

Later that morning in class, Mrs. James said, "Okay, boys and girls, clear your desks. Our guest speaker will be here any minute." Luke stuffed everything into his desk and waited. Mrs. James talked about this bucketfilling subject often since the school year began. He already knew that a bucketfiller does and says nice things. And a bucketdipper doesn't. When we're happy and feeling good, our buckets are full. When we're sad, lonely or angry, our buckets are empty. Luke put his head down on his desk and thought about Marcus. *He's a bucketfiller for sure,* he thought. He looked up for a moment. He didn't see any bucketfillers in the room except Mrs. James. And Bobby. Bobby ate lunch with Luke sometimes, but only when Tim, Bobby's best friend, was absent.

The door opened, and in walked a woman. "Good morning!" she said with a big smile. "My name is Miss Darcy, and we're going to spend the next 90 minutes talking about bucketfilling, your lives and your choices." Miss Darcy asked questions, and most of the students were excited and raised their hands to answer them. They talked about some cool stuff. Luke stayed quiet, but he was listening.

Miss Darcy told the class, "Raise your hand if you believe your bucket is full most of the time." Luke looked around and saw that most of the kids had their hands up. Marcie didn't.

Many of the girls were mean to Marcie because she talked funny. It was hard to understand her. And Joel didn't have his hand up. Some of the kids said that Joel's mom had moved far away and he never saw her. He was always in a bad mood, and sometimes he was a bully. Luke kept his hand down, too.

"Luke," Miss Darcy said. He almost jumped when she spoke his name. "I noticed you did not raise your hand. Does that mean you have an empty bucket most of the time?"

Luke fidgeted in his chair and thought about that. "I guess so," he answered softly.

"If you wouldn't mind, Luke, would you please tell us the feeling you often have that lets you know your bucket is empty? Only if you want to share." Miss Darcy stood in front of Luke and smiled at him.

Luke hated talking in front of other people, but this time he felt like doing it anyway. *This answer will be easy,* he thought.

"I feel left out," he stated.

"And how do you *feel* inside when you're 'left out'?" she asked him.

"Very sad," replied Luke. The speed of his answer surprised him. He didn't even have to think about it.

Then Marcie spoke up suddenly without raising her hand. "I get left out, too," she said. "And then I feel lonely." Tears sprang into her eyes, and she looked down at her desk. Some of the other girls squirmed in their seats and looked away.

Joel raised his hand straight in the air. "What about you, Joel?" Miss Darcy asked.

"I'm angry. I'm real angry every day." And he looked it.

"Thank you," said Miss Darcy. "Thank you so much for your honesty. It's important to know how we are feeling inside. If we don't know the name of the feeling, we certainly can't deal with it."

Miss Darcy went on. "I have a promise for all of you, especially those who shared that their buckets are often empty. If you listen well during this workshop and then *do* what I know will work, I *promise* that your buckets will be full this evening. And that is just the beginning. If you continue to do the simple things we talk about this morning, I *promise* that your buckets will be full much more than they are empty."

Luke was listening; it sounded impossible. Would his arthritis go away? *No.* Would he walk normally? *No.* Would the other kids want to play with him? *No.* But he listened.

The key to having a full bucket is to be a bucketfiller. That was "it." *Sounds simple,* thought Luke. *Too simple.*

"Now it's time for all you to experience 'intensive bucketfilling,'" said Miss Darcy. She explained that *intensive* in this case meant *powerful.* All the students got a piece of paper that read *Why I Love and Respect You* at the top. Then there was a blank after that. She asked them each to choose one person whom they loved and respected, write that individual's name in the blank, and then write at least 10 specific reasons *why* they loved and respected him or her.

"Please be specific. What does this person say or do that is special to you? We'll take about eight minutes. Please be very still and start writing."

Wow, thought Luke. *This is weird.* He had never thought about why he loved people in his life. He just loved them. There were Mom and Dad, of course. *They're both cool. I could write lots of reasons why I love them,* he thought. But then Marcus' face appeared right in front of Luke, almost as if he was really there. *Yeah . . . Marcus!*

Luke bent over his paper and began to write. As he wrote, Luke began to feel differently than he usually did in school. He wasn't worried about what the other kids thought of him or how he looked when he walked. He just thought about Marcus and all the great things he did and said. It startled Luke to realize he even felt like he was going to cry. He jerked his head up for a moment and looked around. Most of the students were busy writing. Everyone looked serious, and no one was talking. Luke wrote more. He pictured Marcus in his mind—how he looked and the things he said.

"Okay, time is up," said Miss Darcy. The students all put their pencils down, and then Miss Darcy asked for volunteers who would like to stand and share with the class what they wrote. Ten students raised their hands to volunteer. Luke did not. But he listened as his classmates read. Madison read hers to her mom. Andy wrote to his dad. He read it aloud although it was really hard to hear him. Luke was surprised that Andy shared, because Andy almost never talked. But his dad was a soldier, and Andy was really proud of that. Then something happened that made the entire class fall completely silent. Joel raised his hand.

"Thank you, Joel," said Miss Darcy. He stood up. Luke looked at Mrs. James. She had been sitting at her desk, dabbing her eyes with a tissue. But when Joel stood to read his list, she clasped her hands in front of her and stared in surprise.

"I wrote to my dad," said Joel in a strong voice. He read several things on his list. Then he said, "Number four. You miss Mom, too, but you always stay strong for me." And then Joel stopped. He put his head down and sniffed. Everyone could see that he was crying. He tried to read more, but he coughed and couldn't speak. Miss Darcy put her arm around him and thanked him. Joel sat down.

All of a sudden Luke raised his hand. He wasn't sure why he did it; he just did.

"Luke, please read yours." Miss Darcy smiled. Luke cleared

his throat. He didn't look up. He knew if he saw all those kids looking at him, he wouldn't be able to read.

"Why I Love and Respect You, Marcus," he began. Luke could feel tears stinging his eyes, but he fought them back. *I want to finish*, he thought, *I want to finish.*

- You always smile at me
- You care about my feelings
- You stick up for me all the time
- You don't care if I limp
- You let me shoot baskets with you and your friends
- You never call me names when you're mad at me
- You let me play your video games
- When you make a sandwich you give me half
- You think it's okay when Mom and Dad and me yell "Marcus!" at your games
- You always tell me the truth

Luke stopped. That was all he wrote. He sat down without looking up. Miss Darcy said, "Thank you, Luke. You obviously have a great brother. Will you read that to him?"

Luke kind of stiffened up inside. *Would he be able to read it to Marcus?* "Probably not," he answered quietly.

"That's okay, but why would you choose to not read it to Marcus?" asked Miss Darcy. Luke thought. He thought hard. *Yeah, why not?*

"Because I think he'll laugh," said Luke. He meant that. *Marcus is 16 years old, and he'll think this is dumb. And then he'll laugh,* Marcus worried.

"It is your choice," said Miss Darcy. "But Luke, please consider the possibility that Marcus might not laugh. He might feel that what you've written is very important, like he obviously thinks you are." Miss Darcy smiled.

After school, Luke sat in his room. He looked at the list he had written to Marcus. Marcus wasn't home yet. He had extra basketball practice because there was a game that night. He and his mom and dad would be there. Luke thought he would leave the list in Marcus' room for him to read that night. Then Luke wouldn't know when he read it. Luke wouldn't know what Marcus thought of this love stuff, and that would be good. Luke opened his bedroom door and started down the hallway toward Marcus' room.

Then he heard "MOM!" It was Marcus! Why was he home? Luke went downstairs to see his brother.

"How come you're home? I thought you had practice," asked Luke.

"Yeah, we did," answered Marcus. "But Coach Smithfield sent us home. Said we should eat something and relax. Said it was more important than practice. This game is big." Marcus was rummaging in the refrigerator. He didn't look at Luke. Luke nervously crumpled the list in his hand.

"So what are you doing anyway?" asked Marcus.

"Nothing," said Luke.

"Well, what's in your hand? Homework?" asked Marcus as he stuffed cheese into his mouth.

"Uh . . . no," said Luke, pretending to search for something in the refrigerator.

"So what is it?" asked Marcus.

"Just something. For you, I guess," answered Luke quietly.

"Oh yeah? Like what?" asked Marcus, tearing open a bag of potato chips.

Luke thought maybe he'd go upstairs to his room. He felt very nervous and uncomfortable. Perhaps he should change into different clothes for the game. After all, he had had this shirt on all day.

"Luke, I'm talking to you, man. What's up?"

"Nothing. Just have this paper," said Luke. *Wow, that was stupid,* thought Luke. *Now he'll ask what it is.*

"What paper?" asked Marcus. *You knew he'd ask that,* thought Luke.

"Oh, just something I wrote," said Luke. "For you, I guess."

"Oh yeah? Cool. Read it," smiled Marcus, crunching on chips and waiting.

How did this happen, Luke thought. *All I was going to do was leave this thing in his room! Now what will I do?* Luke stared at the floor and said nothing.

"Okay, well, I've got to change for the game," said Marcus. "So I'll see you over there, right?" he asked his brother.

"Yeah. Well, wait a minute, Marcus," said Luke, surprised at himself. "Let me read you something." *Oh, my gosh. What in the heck am I doing?* thought Luke.

"Okay. But make it fast. I've got to go," stated Marcus.

Luke cleared his throat. He opened the paper and tried to smooth out the wrinkles. Marcus looked at him and waited. Luke stared at the paper.

"Okay, so what's going on?" asked Marcus. "Come on, Luke, I'm in a hurry!"

Luke finally started to read.

"Why I Love and Respect You, Marcus." Luke read them all, numbers 1 through 10. He only looked up at Marcus once, briefly. Marcus was staring at Luke, just staring. But he didn't smile. And he didn't say a word.

"Is that it?" asked Marcus quietly. Luke could tell that Marcus didn't know what to say, so he said, "Is that it?"

"Well, yeah, that's it," said Luke.

"Okay, cool. Thanks. Well, I've got to get going," said Marcus. But he sat for another second looking at Luke. Luke looked back at Marcus; he had a weird look on his face, one that Luke had never seen before. His eyes were kind of shiny, like he had tears in them. And then he ran upstairs.

Mom and Dad came home a few minutes later. Marcus caught a ride with friends to the game. After dinner, Luke and his parents drove to the school. They climbed the crowded bleachers and sat down. Luke had that excited feeling, like he always did right before one of his brother's games. For some reason, Luke felt really good. He knew the team would win. He could feel it. The game began. Marcus was in, like he usually was. He was a starter. Luke was proud of that. Marcus was co-captain of the team, too. And Luke could tell that when the cheerleaders were jumping around and yelling, they were yelling for Marcus. All of them liked him. Every single one of them.

At halftime, the home team was ahead by only two points. Luke actually never cared who won. He knew he should care, but he didn't. What he cared about was Marcus. Marcus was a great player, and he played a lot. He had sunk several baskets, as usual, and Luke was screaming his lungs out. That's all that mattered.

Right before the second half began, there was silence. A voice boomed over the loudspeaker. "Player number 42, junior Marcus Norman, wants to dedicate this game to his brother, Luke Norman!" Luke could not believe his ears. His parents looked at him. They looked surprised. His mom smiled, and his dad winked at him. Then they turned to the game after the tip-off and yelled "Take it away!" The rest was a blur. Did the team win? Luke did not remember unless he really thought about it hard. What he did remember was how his brother looked at him in the bleachers and gave him a "thumbs up." *Thumbs up for love,* thought Luke.

As Luke and his parents drove home that night, Luke remembered the promise that Miss Darcy had made earlier that day. She promised his bucket would be full if he did what she suggested. And he did it! Luke thought about how he was feeling right at that very moment.

"Hey, Luke," said his dad from the driver's seat. He was grinning, looking at Luke in the rearview mirror. "I hardly recognize you, boy. If you don't stop smiling so big, your face is going to cramp up."

And he, Luke's mom and Luke laughed almost all the way home.

	LET'S TALK ABOUT IT
1	Do you think that Luke had an empty bucket a lot? Name the feelings you think he had and discuss why.
2	Who were the bucketfillers in Luke's life?
3	Who were the bucketdippers in Luke's life?
4	Why do think Luke loved his brother so much?
5	When Luke read his list to Marcus, how do you think Marcus felt? Did he show his feelings? If not, why not?
6	How did Marcus show his feelings later?
7	Is there anyone in your life like Marcus?

CHAPTER 7

The Soldier

A Bucketfiller Can Be Compassionate

It was raining and cold outside. The American soldier, Corporal Olson, was not enjoying his visit to Belgium. He had always wanted to travel to Europe, but not like this, not during World War II. For over six months now, he spent most nights in a foxhole, a long, narrow hole he dug with his own shovel. This foxhole was called "home" by soldiers. Dark came earlier now, and boredom was rampant. If they were off duty, the men usually retired to their "homes." Olson put up the small tent over his foxhole to keep out the rain, pulled his helmet down over his eyes, and tried to sleep. The raindrops tapped on the tent, and he soon dreamed that he heard his mother's high heels clicking on the kitchen floor.

"Olson!" The soldier jerked awake, shoved his helmet up and looked into the glare of a flashlight.

"Yes, sir, what can I do for you, sir?" Corporal Olson, squinting, recognized the voice of Captain Morse.

"I need you to do a couple things in the tent," said the captain.

"Yes, sir," replied Olson. He was wishing he could finish the dream about his mother—he wanted to see her face. But the tent, set up as a temporary office for Captain Morse and Olson, the company clerk, might be a little warmer than this cold dirt. Perhaps he would dry out a little in the tent. Tomorrow they would be on the move again, ordering 40 prisoners into trucks built to hold 24; then they would proceed, several days behind the infantry advancing along the front. The Americans and Allies were winning many battles. It was expected that the war would end soon.

Morse and Olson trudged through patches of weeds and mud to the tent. They passed foxholes as they walked. A few of his buddies were playing cards by flashlight; Olson could see the glow beneath the tiny tents and hear talking; some were obviously sleeping or trying to sleep. The rest were stationed around the temporary enclosure, guarding their prisoners of war.

Olson pulled the flap back on the tent to allow Captain Morse to enter ahead of him. Private Dombrowski was inside. He saluted them and left. Lanterns illuminated the small canvas room. A portable table, used as a makeshift desk, was in the center of the room. The captain's cot, small and narrow, was set up on one side. A large metal box containing files and supplies lay on the floor next to the table. On it were several neat stacks of papers and a shiny, black Remington typewriter. It was Olson's typewriter, issued to him by the U.S. Army, and it was his serious responsibility to keep it safe.

The memory of landing on the beach at Normandy, France, flashed through his mind. His company arrived on June 10, 1944—four days after 100,000 American and Allied soldiers stormed the beaches in a major offensive against the Germans. The goal: To free Europe. More than 9,000 men lost their lives as they arrived on the beaches.

By the time Olson jumped from the landing craft into the waist-deep seawater, the shelling and gunfire had moved inland. He held his Remington typewriter on top of his head with both hands to protect it from getting wet. As he waded in the cold water and kept his balance in the surf, Olson heard Captain Morse's voice above the noise of the waves: "OLSON! DON'T GET THAT TYPEWRITER WET!"

He will always remember his thought at that moment: *Hey, how can I single-handedly win this war with a wet typewriter?*

He used that precious machine to type all the reports necessary for the entire company. There were plenty of reports to be done, too, since Olson and his fellow soldiers were picking up thousands of German prisoners as the Americans and their allies advanced along the front, taking back towns that had been captured earlier by the Germans. By the end of this assignment Olson, his 111 fellow soldiers and three officers would have transported over 225,000 German prisoners across Europe. He typed many ribbons completely dry. It amused Olson when he realized that although food rations often ran low, there were always plenty of fresh typewriter ribbons on hand.

Totally out of place, opposite Morse's cot stood a young prisoner of war. He held an unloaded rifle high over his head with both hands. His wet hair was plastered onto his forehead. His uniform was also wet, and he wore no boots or stockings. The German did not look at Morse or Olson; he stared straight ahead.

Oh, wonderful, thought Olson. *Now I'm not only a clerk, I'm a guard.*

He reached down and instinctively touched the holster that held his Army-issued Colt .45 handgun. He thought back to General Eisenhower's proclamation to the American troops regarding their attitude toward Germans. They were ordered to assume the attitude of conquerors, not oppressors. But they should not speak with the enemy nor associate with them in any way.

Olson almost smiled. *The Germans are slowly retreating, we're whipping them in every battle, and the war will probably end soon. I am almost as wet as this fellow, we're both exhausted. Do I feel like an oppressor or a conqueror?* he wondered. But Olson was an obedient soldier. So he shot the German a stern look, just in case he might glance in Olson's direction.

"Okay, Olson, here's the deal. According to a guard, this guy was uncooperative. So he's here for a few hours to learn a lesson. He understands a few words of English; he knows he's to stand here holding that rifle in the air until I give him permission to put it down. It's been an hour so far. Maybe an all-nighter will help him feel more cooperative when we bug out of here tomorrow." The captain snapped up his rain slicker. "I'll be back in a few hours. I'm taking the Jeep on ahead to check on some things. So keep your eye on him. Got it?"

"Yes, sir. I'll finish up these intake reports while you're gone, sir," Olson said.

"Fine. Be back as soon as I can," said Morse. He turned and left the tent.

Olson looked at the German, who still stared straight ahead and held the rifle high.

Big deal, nine pounds, thought Olson as he looked at the empty rifle. *He can last.*

Olson, the American, felt satisfied that he was thinking in a cool and aloof, but not oppressive, way. General Eisenhower would be pleased. He pulled the chair back from the desk and sat down. He unstrapped his holster, just in case he might need his gun. Then he looked at the stack of papers and tried to remember where he had stopped working earlier that day. He laid his hand on them and looked up at the German soldier. Olson guessed him to be more of a boy than a man, probably 18 years old or so. The Germans had started to call 16-year-olds into service, so maybe this kid was even younger.

Olson thought of his little brother, Kenneth, back home in Chicago. Kenneth was a junior in high school, studying during the day and going home to Mom at night, just as he should be doing. He was on the baseball team and had a girlfriend.

"How old are you?" Olson asked the German. "You speak English?"

The soldier pretended to ignore him and held his arms a bit straighter and higher.

"Sixteen or 17?" Olson pressed for an answer. *Wow, some interrogation,* he thought. *I'm a tough guy, all right.* A couple of minutes went by. The German shifted his bare feet a bit closer together. He coughed, then cleared his throat.

"Seventeen," he said without looking at Olson.

I wonder if he even finished school, thought Olson. He again looked at the kid's wet hair. There were big, dark circles under his eyes. He looked to be underweight, too. It was rumored the Germans were running low on provisions.

Olson wondered if this kid had a family in Germany somewhere. *Probably,* he thought. *Probably parents, if they were still alive, and maybe sisters and brothers. And this kid got yanked out of school, stuck into a uniform and sent out to fight the Americans.*

Olson noticed that the soldier's arms were starting to quiver, just a little. He realized how much he hated being a guard. He wondered what General Eisenhower or General Patton would do at a time like this and nervously tapped his hand on the desk.

"Down," he said.

For the first time, the German looked at Olson, but he didn't move.

"Arms," said Olson. "Put your arms down." Olson pantomimed his instructions to the German, putting his own arms up high and then lowering them.

The enemy soldier gave Olson a quizzical look and then slowly lowered his arms. The last half of the motion went suddenly faster, and Olson reached for his gun. But he quickly realized the German's speed was because of exhaustion, not aggression.

"Drop it," instructed Olson.

The kid dropped the gun at his feet.

The two young men looked at each other. They didn't look at each other's uniform or notice that they were about the same height and they both had blonde hair. They looked into each other's eyes. Neither of them moved for some seconds.

Olson thought of his buddies outside in their foxholes. He thought of the more than half a million American casualties from this war and all the suffering of their loved ones at home. The Germans had started it. Hitler was to blame. Olson thought of General Patton's statement, "The only good German is a dead German!" Olson remembered he and the soldiers around him had cheered loudly when they heard that famous war cry. He again looked at his prisoner and thought, *So would this kid be a better German if he were dead?* Olson was starting to feel guilty.

"Up!" he said to the German soldier. He motioned for the kid to pick the rifle up, which he did.

"Arms up!" Olson ordered. *He's rested long enough,* he

thought. *Darn German.* But even as Olson thought it, he knew he was lying to himself. *He's a kid. Just a kid, doing what he was told to do. He's tired, scared and doing his best to look tough. Just like me.*

"I said, 'UP'!" shouted Olson. He startled himself with his own fierce tone.

The German raised the rifle high above his head and stood very still. Olson went back to looking at the stack of forms he should finish. He felt troubled, but tried to shake it off.

"How old you?" said the German prisoner, quietly.

"What?" asked Olson, shocked that the young man spoke to him.

"You . . . how old?" he asked again, looking at Olson directly.

"Uh, twenty-two," replied Olson.

The prisoner stared straight ahead again.

"Why?" Olson asked the German. "Why do you want to know?"

The German replied, "Why YOU want to know?"

Olson thought, *What is this? A regular conversation?* If Captain Morse heard this chatter, he'd throw Olson in the brig along with the German.

"Up!" commanded Olson. "Keep the rifle up and your mouth closed!" He looked nervously at his watch. The captain had been gone for only 20 minutes. At this rate, it would take forever to get back to his foxhole. In spite of the night's chill, he began to sweat. He looked at his prisoner, whose arms were beginning to quiver again.

"Okay, down," said Olson again. The prisoner looked at him quickly and then looked away.

He slowly lowered the rifle.

"Drop it?" he asked.

"Yeah, yeah, drop it," replied Olson. The gun fell to the dirt floor at the German's feet. He moved back one step to get his toes out from beneath the gun. Olson thought of how good it felt to lie down in his foxhole after being on the move all day. He pointed at the ground in front of the German.

"Sit!" he said.

The young prisoner opened his eyes wide in surprise but stood very still.

"Sit!" repeated Olson, louder this time. He thought, *Captain is right. This guy is uncooperative.*

The German bent his knees and slowly sat down. Olson could see that the kid was stiff, and he grunted a little as he crossed his legs in front of him. Olson got up and walked over to the prisoner. He picked up the rifle and put it on the other side of the tent. Then he sat down at the desk again and picked up a stack of papers. He grabbed the first one and rolled it into the typewriter.

"Why?" asked the German, looking up at Olson.

Olson ignored the question and started to type.

"Sit," said the prisoner. "Why?"

Olson thought, *Yes, why? Good question.* He looked at the German's face. *What will he go home to? Is his family alive?* Olson glanced at his watch and figured the time difference so he could imagine what Kenneth might be doing at this moment. *It's Saturday,* he thought. *Back home, it's lunch time. He probably just finished a sandwich that Ma made him.* He pictured Kenneth sitting at the kitchen table chewing a ham sandwich. Maybe cheese on it, too.

Olson pictured Ma chopping vegetables at the counter, probably for stew that evening. She was humming one of those old Swedish tunes her mother taught her. She had let the cat into the house, which Dad hated. He must be gone somewhere. The cat was purring and making a slow figure-eight as she rubbed against Ma's ankles. His daydreaming was interrupted by a noise coming from the German. Olson looked from his watch to the young man in front of him.

The prisoner had fallen over to his side. His eyes were closed. Olson watched him for any signs of movement. Slowly, the German's legs stretched out, and he moved an arm under his head. *Asleep,* thought Olson. *Just like that. Asleep.* For about a minute, he watched the kid and listened to his steady breathing.

Then Corporal Olson turned his attention back to his reports. For several hours, he heard only the tapping of his typewriter as he listened carefully for the sound of a returning Jeep.

	LET'S TALK ABOUT IT
1	How do think Corporal Olson felt about being a soldier in the war? Name all the feelings you believe he had.
2	What were the feelings that Corporal Olson had toward the German soldier? Why?
3	Did Corporal Olson choose to be a bucketfiller or a bucketdipper? Was it easy for him to make that choice?
4	How do you think the German soldier felt about Corporal Olson?
5	Do you think after the war was over that Corporal Olson and the German soldier remembered each other? Was it a good memory or a bad one?
6	What did you learn from this story?

CHAPTER 8

The Breakfast

Bucketfilling Can Be Fun

It was drizzling and chilly outside, and Gladys didn't feel like going out for breakfast. But she promised Margaret she would meet her at Barnaby's Grill at 9:00 A.M. Like Gladys always said to her children and grandchildren as they were growing up, "A promise is a promise!" So she rummaged through her closet for her black shoes and decided she would drive to Barnaby's whether she felt like it or not.

What would Margaret say if Gladys didn't show up? *Why, she'd be mighty disappointed in me,* thought Gladys. *She's tired of me feeling sorry for myself. She told me I had better just get out there and do something with my days instead of moping around the house!*

Margaret understood how Gladys was feeling since her husband, George, died 18 months ago. Being a widow herself, Margaret knew about grief. But what made it even worse was just as Gladys was beginning to feel alive again, her 15-year-old cat, Charley, got hit by a car on the Old Farm Road. The postal carrier had seen Charley lying on the side of the road and called the police. Deputy Potter drove out and picked up the long-haired, black cat, saw his name tag and gave Gladys a call. That bad news sent Gladys right back into the pits again, and she just wasn't quite ready to climb out.

First George, then Charley, Gladys thought as she struggled to get to sleep each night. Then she would cry.

Gladys put her shoes on, grabbed her hand bag and stepped into the garage. There was George's pride and joy—the shiny, black Chevrolet that he bought just before he got sick. "My, how he loved that car!" Gladys would say to Margaret.

Gladys backed the Chevrolet carefully out of the garage, pushed the button to close the door and started off to Barnaby's. She turned on the windshield wipers. They squeaked with each swipe. *Oh, I hate that sound!* thought Gladys. She knew if she turned the wipers off, she wouldn't be able to see through the water, so she decided to put up with the squeaking. *It's a short ride, anyway,* she mumbled to herself. *Thank goodness!*

Barnaby's new sign was bright red with yellow lettering. None of the regular customers understood why the new owners changed it. The old one was just fine, and this one looked like some cheap motel out on the highway. But the food was still good, so most of the regulars kept coming, especially on Saturday mornings like today. There were great specials, and when you figure that along with the senior citizens discount, you got yourself a bargain.

Gladys pulled into the parking lot and looked for a wide space. She preferred the ones on the end of the row so she could open her door as far as she wanted. There was one available, so she took it.

Right after she pulled into the space, another car took the space right across from her. It was a blue van, and before the vehicle was still for even a second, the side door slid open. Three young boys popped out like they had been shot from a cannon, pushing each other and laughing loudly. A woman

Gladys thought to be their mother opened her door, and then the driver, a man, opened his.

"Calm down, you guys," said the woman. "Remember, we're going into a public place. Try not to embarrass us!" and she smiled at the man. The man said, "Do what your mother says!" and grinned at her. As Gladys opened her door to step out, the man, presumably the father, let out a loud belch. The boys laughed and yelled, "Way to go, Dad!"

"Mike, you're such a great example to your sons," groaned the mother sarcastically, and she swatted him on the behind. The boys ran ahead to the restaurant door and waited.

Gladys sat in the driver's seat with the door open. She watched as the family made its way into the restaurant. She thought, *That behavior is disgusting. It's a good thing George isn't here right now. If our children had acted that way, we would have turned around and gone right home. No breakfast for them! And George—I don't think I heard him burp like that in all the 52 years I was married to him. And in public! What is happening to young people nowadays?*

Gladys was grateful that she moved slowly so she likely wouldn't be waiting for a table at the same time as that rowdy bunch. *Please, let them sit far away from me!* she thought.

Walking into Barnaby's alone, or any place for that matter, was difficult for Gladys. George always held her arm, opened doors for her, and told the hostesses in restaurants, "Table for two, please." She felt secure being with George. Now she was by herself. She felt as though people stared at her when she entered a place all alone. But Gladys realized this was in her own head—probably no one took notice of her. She entered the door of Barnaby's and walked up to the hostess.

"Table for two, please," said Gladys as she looked around for Margaret. She wasn't there yet. *Whoever gets there first, get a table* was their rule. The hostess asked Gladys, "Do you mind sitting at the back of the restaurant? All the other tables are taken."

"Oh, no, that would be fine," replied Gladys, happy to be farther away from people. She also glanced around to see where the rowdy family was sitting. There they were, on the far left and toward the front. The boys were squirming in their chairs and grabbing at each other's menus. *Good, I'll be far from them!* thought Gladys.

She sat down in the booth facing the door. That way, she and Margaret would easily see each other. The hostess handed her a menu and said, "Your waitress will be right with you." Gladys kept the menu folded in front of her. *I will order coffee and wait for Margaret,* she thought, staring at the door. *Margaret, please hurry, dear.*

"I mean it, you guys, sit still!" said Suzanne to her three rambunctious sons. They stopped wiggling and looked at their menus. Rory had his upside down.

"Okay, you three," said Mike, their dad. "Decide what you want to eat, but you know the main reason we've come. Tell us what you're going to order, and then start looking around."

"Right, Dad," said Michael Jr., the oldest boy. Michael was a fourth-grader at Bixby Elementary School. His younger brothers, Zack and Rory, looked up to their older brother. Zack was in second grade and Rory in kindergarten. "Come on, Squirts, you know why we're here."

"Yeah!" replied Rory. He started banging the toe of his shoe against the pedestal of the table.

Zack said, "Rory, stop! You just kicked me!"

"Did not! I kicked the table," said Rory.

Mike spoke to his sons, sternly this time. "Boys, that's it. We all want pancakes, right?" They nodded affirmatively. "Okay, pancakes it is. Want bacon or sausage?"

"No," replied Rory.

"No, THANK YOU," said Zack, looking at his younger brother with disapproval.

The waitress stopped at their table, holding her order pad. "What can I get for you?" she asked with a smile.

"Well," said Suzanne. "May we wait just a few minutes? We have something else to decide."

"Of course," she replied. "Take your time. I'll be back with coffee." She left.

"So, boys, what do you think? Have you looked around?" asked Mike. "Who shall we pick?"

Michael replied, "I've been looking around, but everyone looks happy, Dad."

"Not everyone is happy!" said Zack loudly. "I'm too hungry to be happy!"

"Me too!" said Rory.

Michael craned his neck around and looked toward the back of the restaurant. "Wait a minute," he whispered. "There is a lady sitting way in the back. She doesn't look very happy. In fact, she looks like she's going to cry any minute."

Gladys fidgeted with her menu. The waitress was walking her way again. After drinking a cup of coffee, Gladys was wondering if Margaret would get there at all. She thought, *Perhaps I should order now. I don't think I can stand sitting here alone for much longer. Come on, Margaret! This outing was your idea, after all.* The waitress asked, "Are you still waiting for your friend, ma'am?"

"Well, yes, I am, but I think I'll go ahead and order." Gladys realized then that she hadn't decided on anything yet, nor had she even put her reading glasses on. She hastily ordered what George usually ordered, and handed the menu to the waitress.

Margaret, where are you? Gladys thought, and she wished she could be at home instead of alone in this restaurant.

"Oh, yes, I see her," said Suzanne to her family. "She's sitting alone, way in the back. Look, Mike, the woman with the gray hair and dark sweater."

"Yes, I'm looking at her, but I'm trying not to be obvious about it," replied her husband.

"Boys, do you see her?" Mike asked his younger sons.

The waitress set Gladys' breakfast plate on the table. There it was. Gladys hadn't seen a Belgian waffle since the last time she and George were here. It was his favorite thing to order at Barnaby's. It was huge, with fresh strawberries piled in the middle and a dollop of whipped cream on top of it all.

"Would you care for anything else?" asked the waitress.

"No, thank you. But you can remove the other place setting. I don't think my friend will be here this morning," Gladys said.

Why did I ask her to do that? It doesn't really matter. But Gladys knew she was feeling hurt and a bit angry at Margaret. Why hadn't she shown up? *Doesn't Margaret realize how awkward this is for me?* Gladys thought. She kept her head down and pushed the strawberries around on top of the waffle. *Should I put syrup on it, like George did?* she asked herself. Gladys decided that would be much too sweet. She began to eat even though her appetite was small.

Young Michael said softly, "Well, you guys, I think she's the one." He turned back to his family after looking at Gladys, and smiled a huge smile. Mike, Suzanne, Zack and Rory smiled back at him and began to dig into their pancakes. Michael spread butter on his and thought back to what had happened in school the day before.

At 9:30 A.M., a guest walked into their classroom. She was there to present a workshop about Bucketfilling. Michael already knew what it meant to be a bucketfiller; they had talked about it in class. A bucketfiller is a person who says and does kind things. Michael told his mom after school that he would always remember the things the speaker said. What impressed Michael the most was the story she told right at the end of the workshop. It was a true story that had happened to her father over 25 years ago. He and his wife were having breakfast at a restaurant. When they finished eating, he asked the waiter for the check so he could pay for the meals. The waiter said, "Your food has already been paid for." The speaker's dad said, "What do you mean it's paid for? I haven't paid yet."

The waiter said, "Yes, I know. Did you notice the young woman in the booth next to you?"

The young woman had already left, but the man said, "Yes, I noticed her. Why?" "She paid for your breakfasts," the waiter said. "And she asked me to tell you this: 'It's a random act of kindness, pass it on.'" The speaker said her father was surprised and very impressed by the kind thing the young woman had done.

He took what she said very seriously, and he passed on her bucketfilling act many times during the next 25 years. He thought perhaps he had bought breakfast or lunch for a stranger at least 100 times. He always asked the waiter or wait-ress to not tell the person he had done it. "Just tell them," he said, "it's a random act of kindness, pass it on."

The speaker wondered how many people had gotten their buckets filled in that way, by a total stranger, just because of that one young woman 25 years ago. She called it a "ripple effect." Michael wondered, too. He thought and thought about that. He even used a calculator to try to figure it out. He got lost in the thousands somewhere.

When he explained the story to his mother, he said, "Wow, Mom, that's not just a ripple. That's a tidal wave!"

"You like that idea, don't you?" asked his mother.

"Yes! I think it would be awesome to start our own ripple effect. Could we, Mom?"

"I think that's a great idea. I'll talk to your father about it when he gets home from work."

"Okay!" replied Michael, and he ran upstairs to tell his little brothers about bucketfilling.

That evening after they finished dinner, Mike asked his fami-ly to remain at the table for a few minutes. He then proposed that they go out for breakfast the next morning and do a ran-dom act of kindness. "This is Michael's idea," he said, patting his oldest son on the back. "And I think it's terrific. Now, I can certainly afford to buy a person's breakfast; but since you guys want to be part of this, how about contributing some of your own money? Your mom and I don't care how much. It can even be nothing, if that's your choice. Just decide if you want to contribute, and if you do, put your money on my nightstand before you jump into bed. What do you say?"

"All right!" replied Michael, grinning from ear to ear.

"Count me in!" said Zack.

"Can I stay up later tonight if I give you some dimes?" asked Rory.

Mike swept his young son into his arms, kissed him on the cheek and slung him over his shoulder. "Absolutely not!" he replied as he took Rory upstairs to tuck him into bed.

That night when Suzanne and Mike went into their room to go to bed, they found a dollar bill, three quarters and four dimes on Mike's nightstand.

Gladys had eaten about half of the waffle. She didn't think she could put even one more bite into her mouth. It was so sweet! *George always had such a sweet tooth,* she thought. Gladys laid her fork down on the plate, took the napkin from her lap and dabbed at the corners of her mouth. *George, how I miss you! If you were here, I wouldn't be waiting and worrying about Margaret.* Tears sprang to her eyes. Gladys cleared her throat. *Stop that!* She ordered herself. *Just stop it!*

"May I take your plates if you're finished?" the waitress asked Mike, Suzanne and the boys.

"Yes, please," answered Mike. "And we'll take our check now, too."

"Dad! Don't forget about you-know-who!" Michael whispered loudly.

"Yeah, Dad," added Zack.

"Daddy! Did you bring our money?" shouted Rory.

"Ssssshhhh!" hissed Michael. "Do you want her to hear us? It's a secret! She's not supposed to know who did it!"

"Okay, guys, simmer down," said Mike. He turned back to the waitress, who still stood by their table with their plates in her hands, looking a bit confused.

Suzanne held her finger to her lips, signaling the boys to be quiet.

"Do you see that older woman sitting way back there?" Mike asked the waitress.

She turned around and scanned the back of the restaurant. "The one sitting alone?"

"Yes, that one. We'd like to buy her breakfast. Would you please sneak her check over to us? Don't tell her we're paying for it, though. Just tell her . . . tell her. . . ." Mike pretended he couldn't remember the rest.

"Tell her, 'It's a random act of kindness, pass it on,'" said Michael, pronouncing every word very carefully as he looked at the waitress.

"Oh. All right." She smiled at Michael. "I'll be right back with both of your checks."

Rory and Zack had turned around in their chairs and were looking at the woman.

"You guys, cut it out. She's going to guess it's us!" warned Michael.

Suzanne told her family, "I don't even think she knows about it yet. The waitress hasn't gone over there. I'll tell you when she does." Suzanne was facing that way and could glance up without being obvious. The boys ducked their heads and covered their mouths with anticipation.

Gladys regained her composure and pushed her plate away. Her waitress walked over and took it. "Would you like anything else, or should I bring your check now?" she asked.

"No, no. I've have plenty. Just bring me the check, please." said Gladys. She sighed and opened her purse. She pulled out her wallet and waited.

The two waitresses talked to each other in hushed tones at the cash register. Gladys' waitress gave her check to the other waitress, who walked it over to Mike and his family. Mike pulled his wallet out of his back pocket and counted out money for both checks.

"Look! Look! The lady's waitress is gonna tell her!" said Zack excitedly.

"Ssshhhh!" hissed Michael.

Suzanne said, "Okay, her waitress is talking to her now."

"Do you have my check?" Gladys asked the waitress, who was just standing at the table saying nothing.

"No ma'am, I don't. Your breakfast is already paid for."

"What?" asked Gladys, looking up for the first time since she arrived at the restaurant. "What do you mean?"

"I mean someone already paid for it. And I am supposed to tell you something," said the waitress shyly.

"Tell me what?" asked Gladys. She took a quick look around the restaurant for Margaret. Had Margaret come in and decided to play a joke on her? But Margaret was not there.

"I am supposed to tell you, 'It's a random act of kindness, pass it on,'" replied the waitress, carefully saying the words she was asked to repeat. She smiled at Gladys.

Gladys didn't know what to say. She was shocked. *Who in the world would buy my breakfast?* she asked herself. She looked around the restaurant again and then back at the waitress.

"Please tell me who did this," said Gladys to the waitress.

"I really don't know, ma'am. Gosh, I've never had anything like this happen before," said the waitress to Gladys. "You're really lucky."

"Well, yes," said Gladys. "I suppose I am."

The waitress said, "Have a good day," and walked back into the kitchen.

"Thank you. You, too," mumbled Gladys as she sat at the table with her hands in her lap. She was still holding her wallet. *What a wonderful person, to do something like this!* thought Gladys. She pictured George's face, smiling, and she wondered what he would say at a time like this. Suddenly she knew; she knew as sure as anything exactly what George would say.

Gladys, he'd say, cocking his head to one side and narrowing his eyes at her. *How many times have I told you that people are really good when you give them half a chance? And life is good, too. You just quit this sulking around, Gladys. You'll see me again soon enough. You just get out there in the world and smile, you hear me?*

As Gladys stood up and put her wallet in her purse, she smiled. *Yes, George. I hear you all right.* She walked straight to the front door of the restaurant, her head held higher than when she had walked through it earlier.

Mike, Suzanne, and the boys held their breath as Gladys walked past them. Then Michael said, "Wow, did you see that? She was smiling!"

"She certainly was, Son. I think our ripple effect has begun!" said Mike. He and his family got up and left the restaurant.

Gladys sat behind the wheel of her car feeling very good. She thought of Margaret. *Why, I'm just driving over to her house right now to make sure she's all right. Her memory isn't what it used to be. I'll bet she just forgot about this morning. Then I'll tell her I'm picking her up tomorrow morning and we're going out for breakfast, my treat!*

As Gladys turned the key in the ignition of the shiny Chevrolet, that rowdy family walked past her car to their van. The boys shoved each other, each trying to be the first into the back seat. The mother and father got into the front seat; as they were putting their seat belts on, they looked up at Gladys. Their eyes met for a brief moment. Gladys smiled, gave them a little wave, and they waved back.

Well, really, they're not so bad, thought Gladys, as she slowly backed out of her parking spot.

	LET'S TALK ABOUT IT
1	How do you think Gladys was feeling before she left her house for the restaurant? Why was she feeling that way?
2	How were Mike, Suzanne, Michael, Rory, and Zack feeling when they arrived at the restaurant? Why were they feeling that way?
3	What was the feeling that Gladys had about Margaret when she didn't come to the restaurant?
4	What feelings did Gladys have when she found out someone had paid for her breakfast?
5	Why do you think that Gladys changed her feelings about Margaret after the family filled Gladys' bucket?
6	Why do you think Gladys thought Michael's family wasn't "so bad" at the end of the story? Why did her feelings about them change if she didn't even know they bought her breakfast?

CHAPTER 9

Jason

Can You Recognize the Bucketfillers in Your Life?

When he walked through the front doors of the school, Jason kept his head down. He didn't want to see anyone he knew. They might say "Hi," and he didn't feel like talking. He hated eighth grade. In fact, he hated school. He just felt like hanging out at the apartment and watching television. But he couldn't. Not with the two of *them* there, too.

Jason turned the corner into the hallway that led to his math classroom. After math, it was all downhill. His best grade was always in math, and this semester he had algebra. Many kids thought the formulas were tough to understand. Jason thought that algebra, or math in general, was the only thing in the world that made sense. *Numbers are consistent and never lie,* thought Jason many times. *They are dependable and true. Unlike people.*

Jason walked into math class and sat down. He took the book out of his backpack and slammed it noisily on the desk. A few other kids came in and were talking at the front of the room. The teacher wasn't there yet.

"Hey, Jason," shouted Monty, the guy with probably the biggest mouth in the school. "Where you been, dude?"

Jason looked up at him and said nothing. The girl standing with Monty, Lisa Parker, was the hottest girl in the eighth grade. Jason never could understand why she hung out with Monty. He thought he should answer, just in case Lisa wanted to know, too.

"I been hangin' at home. Why you want to know?" Jason asked.

"Cause you ain't been here in over a week. Teacher been asking about ya," replied Monty.

"Good. Let 'im ask," replied Jason with a scowl. *People are too nosey*, he thought.

Mr. Umber came into the room, followed by more students. The kids took their seats, and Mr. Umber sat on the corner of his desk at the front of the class.

"Good morning, ladies and gentlemen," he said. "And you, too, Monty," he added with a grin. "In case you've forgotten, this morning we're having a special presentation that will take our math time and the time for whatever class you have next. You'll stay in this room for two class periods."

Awesome, thought Jason. *That means I don't have history next hour. Looks like I showed up on a good day.*

Mr. Umber continued. "The speaker should be here any minute. I'd like all of you to clear your desks, except for your name tags. Remember to be respectful to our guest. The principal invited her here to speak about bucketfilling, something most of you are familiar with already; please put your best foot forward."

Monty whispered to Lisa loudly enough for Jason to hear him. "Yeah, I'd like to put my foot someplace, but it ain't forward!" and he laughed like it was the best joke in the world.

Lisa looked at Jason and rolled her eyes. She didn't laugh at Monty.

Monty got on Jason's nerves; he wanted to punch him. He turned around, gave Monty a dirty look, and quickly faced forward again.

Mr. Umber looked at Jason and said, "Jason, it's great to see you back . . . ," but before he could finish what he was about to say, a woman walked into the room.

"Ah, you must be Miss Darcy," said Mr. Umber.

"Yes," said the woman. She smiled, introduced herself and began to write some things on the white board.

She's going to tell us about bucketfilling, thought Jason. *Big deal. Living with a warm and caring heart. What garbage. She probably gets paid to tell us a bunch of stuff that means nothing.* Jason slouched down in his seat and decided to take this time to relax and tune out. While Miss Darcy was talking, Jason thought about what happened that morning at home.

At 4:30 A.M., Jason woke up to some noise. It was too early for his alarm clock, and besides, he hadn't set it the night before. He had already decided to stay home from school again. He'd have the apartment to himself, and Jason liked that. There was no one to tell him what to do and no one to worry about. His mom was gone, as usual. She hadn't been home in a week. Jason didn't like it when she disappeared like that. It never was a good thing when she took off with some guy she just met. He worried about her, but he worried even more when she was at home. He didn't know which was worse: when she was home, or when she was gone.

Mom had been losing lots of weight. She was looking bad. Skinny, bags under her eyes from the booze. And the smoking was getting to her, too. He heard her hacking and coughing when she was home. Sometimes, Jason wanted to yell at her to stop it, to stop the coughing and be quiet. But she never listened to him, and he knew she couldn't help it—unless she quit smoking. And Jason's mom never quit anything except her job, and . . . him.

The noise was Mom stumbling up the steps to their apartment. She was laughing and talking with someone. She fumbled with the door, got it open and Jason heard her and someone else come into the living room where he slept on the floor. He kept his eyes shut and pretended to be asleep. When he heard his mother's bedroom door shut, he sighed.

Mom's alive, he thought. *But now where do I go today? Who wants to be here with them around?* Jason thought he would probably go back to Debbie's house for a few days. It was clean at Debbie's, and she had plenty of food. Debbie used to be good friends with Alice, Jason's mom. But shortly after Jason was born and his father took off, Alice started drinking and doing drugs.

Debbie had come over to see them and found Jason alone in his crib, crying from hunger and needing a diaper change. She took Jason back to her house. When Alice called Debbie all freaked out about where her son went, Debbie told her that she had Jason and to leave him there "until she got her priorities straight." A month later, Alice showed up at Debbie's, sober and wanting to take her baby home. Debbie felt she had to let her take him, but it never lasted for long.

For thirteen years now, Jason went back and forth between his mom and Debbie. When his mom was sober, she was all right and he kind of liked being with her. But when she wasn't sober, which was most of the time; he either stayed home alone or went to Debbie's. Debbie called Jason every day to ask if Alice was at home. As he got older, Jason would lie sometimes and say she was home, just so he could stay alone and skip school.

Debbie never let him skip school when he stayed with her. It was hard to choose where to stay sometimes, because Jason liked the attention that Debbie gave him. She got up early with him and her daughter, Marsha, and made breakfast for them. She even made him take a vitamin every morning, which Jason thought was weird but he took it anyway. Debbie helped him with homework in the evenings and even hugged him goodnight.

When Jason was at his mom's apartment, he would listen for her to come home. He could tell if she was sober by the way it sounded when she walked up the stairs. The first three steps didn't tell him much; he would hold his breath as he listened for the rest. When he was younger, he cried when she was drunk. But now he didn't care so much. At least if she came home, he knew she wasn't dead somewhere. Going to Debbie's meant he couldn't listen for his mom to come home, but after a while he just had to get some good food and hang out with people who talked to him and cared about him.

Debbie's daughter, Marsha, was a year older than Jason. She was cool with him and always wanted him to stay at their house, too. They only had two bedrooms in their small house. He knew that Marsha put guy-stuff like basketball and hockey posters on the walls of her bedroom so that Jason would feel like it was his room, too. She even got rid of the pink stuff in there a few years back, although he never asked her to do that. When he stayed at their house, Marsha would bunk with her mom. He felt weird about that. He said he would sleep on the sofa, but Debbie and Marsha wanted him to "have some privacy."

Although he didn't want to admit it, he liked having his own space. At his mom's there was only one bedroom, and it was hers. He slept on the floor in the living room, which wasn't so bad after he got used to it. The sofa had fallen apart a few years back, and they put it out for the trash collectors. His mom kept promising to get a new one from the secondhand store, but any money she had went for cigarettes, alcohol or drugs.

Yes, Jason thought. He would go to Debbie's tonight and maybe stay for the week. He knew she'd make homemade pizza for him like she always did when he showed up. Jason always told her, "Don't go to no trouble just for me," but down deep he liked it. Jason supposed that Debbie and Marsha were more like an aunt and a cousin than friends, and that made him feel good. Debbie asked Jason many times to stay with them permanently. He didn't know why he always said "no." Sometimes he was there for weeks at a time, but Jason always felt the need to go back to his mom's place for a while. Alice stopped looking for Jason years ago, because she knew he was at Debbie's. But for some reason he still went home to check on her.

Jason's thoughts were interrupted by the speaker. He had done a good job of tuning her out up until now, but something she said got his attention. She said that everyone is in control of their own happiness. Yeah, right. But then Jason heard her say something he had never heard before, and it touched him somewhere in his gut: "Where you come from doesn't decide where you're going—YOU DO." Images came flooding into his mind of daydreams he had been having for a long time about his future. He saw himself sitting around doing nothing, maybe drinking like Mom, probably dropping out of school or getting kicked out again for skipping too many days. It just seemed inevitable. That's what his mom did. And she said she did it because she couldn't help it; her dad did it. And her mom, the grandmother Jason never met, was always complaining and feeling miserable; she wound up leaving Alice and her dad for another guy.

From the time he could remember, Jason figured his life would be similar. But those words, *Where you come from doesn't decide where you are going.* . . . . Could they be true?

"Hey!" said Jason suddenly without putting his hand up. Some of the kids turned around and stared at him.

"I mean, hey, I have a question," said Jason, feeling a little embarrassed.

"Okay, what's your question?" the speaker asked, smiling at him.

"Well, you said we can choose to be happy, that we're in control. Right?"

"Yes," she answered.

"And it don't matter about our family and stuff?"

"Of course, it *matters,* Jason. Family is very important. But you still make your own choices."

"But what if stuff is really bad and you don't know a way out?" Jason asked. His question surprised even him. He usually didn't talk in front of the other kids.

"Everyone deserves a good family life, Jason. But the truth is, many people don't get that. Another truth is that when people with challenging backgrounds become adults, they are held just as accountable for their choices as everyone else."

"Yeah," replied Jason. "So what can you do?"

"I'm not sure, Jason. That is up to each individual. But think of it this way. Let's say you're in a building that you don't like. It is ugly and uncomfortable. You want to get out and find another place that lets you feel safe and comfortable. But when you try to leave, you discover all the doors are locked from the outside. You run from door to door, shaking the doorknobs and pulling on them, but you can't get out. You start to feel frightened and angry because you can't get out. Can you picture that in your mind?" asked the speaker.

"Yeah, I can. It sounds like my life," said Jason.

"So if you were in that situation, what do you think you would do?" Miss Darcy asked.

"Start screaming probably," said Jason. He looked around at some of the other kids in the class. They were completely quiet, listening.

"Would the screaming get you out?" she asked.

"No. But I'd be ticked off and maybe scared," replied Jason.

"Okay, so let's say you scream for a while, and then you get tired of doing that. You're still inside the unpleasant building. Would could you do to get out?"

Jason thought. He could almost feel the panic of being in that place. What would he do? He pictured himself running around the building, wildly looking for some way to escape; he felt his hands get clammy with sweat. *I want to get out!* Then the answer hit him, and he couldn't help smiling in relief.

"A window!" Jason said. "I would find a window and crawl out!" he said triumphantly.

"Very good." she said, walking closer to him. She stood right in front of Jason, and looked into his eyes.

"You see, many times in life we feel that doors are closed to us. And perhaps they are. But when all the doors are closed, Jason, there is always a window. Just find it."

Jason couldn't even speak at that moment. He wasn't sure what all this meant, but he knew it meant something big. He listened to the rest of the presentation, but he continued to picture himself standing on a chair to reach a high window. Jason opened it, jumped onto the edge and crawled through.

On the outside, fresh air filled his lungs, and the grass he lay on felt cool. He saw himself stand up and start walking. The sun was shining; there were other buildings along the street where he walked. He liked most of them, but he kept walking, knowing he was looking for the one that would be perfect for him. *Weird,* thought Jason. *This is weird. But it's cool.*

At the end of the presentation, Miss Darcy gave everyone a piece of paper that had "Why I Love and Respect You" written across the top. There was a blank after that. She said, "Please choose one person you love and respect and write at least 10 specific reasons *why* you love and respect them. This is an exercise not only about love, but about gratitude. We call this *intensive bucketfilling.* Your assignment tonight will be to read your list to the person you chose. Reading it to them rather than just handing it to them will be powerful. You will be filling their bucket, but you will also be filling your own. Expressing love is a great way to keep your bucket full."

Jason looked down at the paper in front of him. He chewed on the end of his pencil and thought. *I should probably write to Mom. I love her, but I just don't know what I'd say.* Jason put his pencil down on the desk and decided he just wouldn't write anything. He started to feel angry as he looked around at the other kids writing. *They're probably writing to their moms and dads and coming up with all this cool stuff they do for them. They should have my life. Then they wouldn't be writing.*

Just a few minutes ago, Jason had been feeling good. Now he was feeling bad. *What is going on?* he thought. He again pictured himself in that awful house, trying to open one of the doors so he could escape. *Out! I've got to get out. . . .* Then, in his mind, Jason looked up and saw a window.

A sudden calm washed over Jason. As the idea came to him, he felt like smiling; then the urge to smile was replaced by the tears that filled his eyes. He quickly wiped them away with his sleeve and grabbed his pencil. In the blank after the words *Why I Love and Respect You,* Jason wrote the name *Debbie.* As he wrote the first thing on the list, he knew that Debbie would ask him what it meant; he would enjoy explaining it to her. Jason wrote, "Debbie, I love and respect you because you are my window."

	LET'S TALK ABOUT IT
1	Why do you think that Jason didn't like going to school?
2	What was missing in Jason's life that caused him to be angry?
3	Who were the bucketfillers in this story?
4	Who were the bucketdippers in this story?
5	In what ways did each bucketfiller help Jason?
6	How do you think Jason was feeling as he wrote to Debbie?
7	Do you think anything changed in Jason's life after he read the list to Debbie?
8	Is your life like Jason's in any way? Do you know anyone like Jason?

CHAPTER 10

The Gym Teacher

Bucketfillers Can Inspire Others to Greatness

Ladies and gentlemen, we have reached our cruising altitude of 38,000 feet . . . ," the flight attendant announced. The rest of what she said droned into nothingness as Fiona's thoughts drifted. *Tokyo,* she thought. *I can't believe I'm going to dance in Japan.*

She leaned toward the window and touched her forehead to it. She felt the slight vibration and heard the humming of the airplane's engines. Sunset. The sun was lowering in the horizon, creating a spectacular orange glow. Fiona thought, *When I wake up, will it really be yesterday? They say we will gain 12 hours. So actually, I'll have an extra 12 hours of life that I wouldn't have had without this trip! Perhaps if the plane keeps flying west fast enough for many days, I could actually be 12 years old again by the time we land.*

"Fiona! Your mind is wandering again, sweet girl. Please focus on your steps!" She could almost hear Mrs. McCrary's words from years ago startling her back to the dance. *Yes,* thought Fiona. *Focus. That still can be a challenge for me, Mrs. McCrary.* She shivered as she contemplated the great adventure ahead of her. "Good-bye, New York. Hello, Tokyo!" she whispered to herself.

Fiona glanced to her right at Lorna, wondering if she had heard that whisper. But Lorna was already dozing. *How can she possibly sleep at a time like this?* Fiona wondered. Her stomach was doing flip-flops! Lorna was experienced in traveling with a dance company, and she had shared stories with Fiona about the trips: Australia, Germany, Italy, even Russia! So perhaps Lorna was relaxed about going to Japan. But not Fiona! This was her first time traveling with a dance company, and she could barely contain her excitement. Clouds below us, she observed. I wonder what state is down there. Indiana, perhaps? She leaned her head back against the headrest and stretched her long legs as far as she could. Fiona looked sideways again at Lorna. Her long, brown hair framed her bare face, the ends curling softly on her shoulders. Her jaw was relaxed in sleep, her mouth slightly opened. *How interesting,* thought Fiona.

How different she and Lorna look now compared to two days ago on stage. Both of them had their long hair pulled back tightly and pinned into a knot at the backs of their heads. Their makeup had taken more than an hour to apply, and their *Best of Broadway* costumes, which drew such applause from the audience, were difficult to get into without assistance. But it was exciting and all so worth it! Dancing on the famous stage at New York City's Carnegie Hall, and then . . . the solo. Fiona's solo! Smile. Breathe. Remember. Focus. Fiona closed her eyes, savoring the memory of that special night just two days ago. At the end, just as the applause was beginning and she was taking a deep bow, she imagined Mrs. McCrary's smiling face. . . .

In the fall of 1963 in Falkirk, Scotland, a city not too far from Glasgow, eight-year-old Fiona had been feeling very low for a long time. Since her parents' divorce, Fiona had lost all of her friends. She knew no one else with divorced parents; the neighbors were shocked and stopped talking to them. The day Fiona's mother left their beautiful home with her daughters, Fiona was frightened and confused. She watched her mother as she packed up all their clothing. Father was away at work, and Mother said they needed to be out of the house before he got home. Fiona wanted to ask why this was happening, but she sensed she should keep quiet. Mum had seemed angry, but she was trying to be patient with her daughters. Fiona was the oldest, and she wanted to be strong for her little sisters.

When Fiona saw Papa during the past few weeks, he would look at her with watery eyes and then look away. *What is wrong?* She wanted to ask him. *Don't you love me anymore?*

As Fiona's mother rushed about the house stuffing things in suitcases, Fiona took a walk down the hallways and peeked into each room. There were ten of them, and everyone said theirs was a grand house. Fiona's friends lived nearby, but they especially loved to play at her house because of all the big rooms. They called the second set of steps to the upstairs off the kitchen their "secret passageway." Fiona trudged up these steps for what she guessed would be the last time. *Must be brave for Claire and Bonnie,* she thought, as she wiped away her tears. Her little sisters really had no idea what was going on. They thought leaving the house was a holiday trip, and they were all smiles. *Mum should tell them about moving to the little apartment and leaving so many things behind,* Fiona thought.

"Mum, tell them we aren't going on holiday," she begged, but her mother shooed her away saying the little ones wouldn't understand. As Fiona sat alone in her room on that last day, she thought, *I don't understand, either.*

The apartment was small and cramped, and they had to walk up two flights of stairs to reach it. All three girls shared the same bedroom. It did not feel like home at all. The only thing that stayed the same was school. Fiona had been en-rolled in one of the best schools in Falkirk; when she took the intelligence test, her score was very high. So although the trip was long, and now in a bus instead of Papa's big, black car, Fiona walked through the same doors of Inverness Park Pri-mary School each morning.

Within a month it became obvious to Fiona that her friends were excluding her. "Mum, why are they doing that? It makes me very sad," Fiona lamented at suppertime.

"Now Fiona, don't complain," her mother answered. "Things are different for all of us, not just you. We don't live in a fancy house anymore, and that's the plain truth of it. No more secret passageway. You'll find other friends." Then her mother cleared the dishes from the table and washed them in silence.

Fiona did not find other friends. She kept to herself most of the time, except for occasionally playing with her little sisters. But Claire and Bonnie whined a lot and weren't much fun. Af-ter they realized the apartment was not a holiday, they began to miss their house and Papa. Fiona missed him, too. Mum wouldn't answer any questions about him, and he never came to see them. The only thing that still gave her pleasure was dance.

Fiona didn't understand how she could still take dance les-sons when they seemed to be so poor now, but she didn't ask about it. *If I ask, the lessons might go away,* she thought. And Fiona felt that if she had to stop dancing, she would die.

When she was 11 years old, Fiona graduated from primary school. The secondary school was larger and had many more students. There Fiona felt some relief from the pressure of at-tending Inverness Park. Although she still hated school and had no friends, at least she felt anonymous. She could isolate herself and be less noticed. But someone noticed her. It was Mrs. McCrary, the gym teacher. Fiona liked her because she was always smiling and friendly. The students respected Mrs. McCrary; they could tell she genuinely loved her job.

One day after gym class, Mrs. McCrary approached Fiona with a smile. "Fiona, do you have a minute?" Fiona had never spoken to Mrs. McCrary, so she felt shy.

"Yes, ma'am," she softly replied.

"Would you be interested in joining our dance company? We meet after school. It's actually lots of fun. What do you think?"

"What kind of dancing?" Fiona asked her teacher.

"Oh, mainly ballet and modern dance. You can make up some of the steps yourself if you like."

"Make them up?" asked Fiona. She was astonished. The teacher at her outside dance class was very strict. They certainly were not allowed to make anything up!

"Yes, sure. Come and see. Please!" Mrs. McCrary said.

"Thank you. I will definitely ask my mum," answered Fiona. For the first time in a long time, Fiona felt like smiling as she traveled home to the little apartment.

"More dancing?" asked her mother that evening.

"Yes, please, Mum! It won't cost any money. Mrs. McCrary, the gym teacher, invites some of the girls who like to dance and even lets them make things up. Can you believe that?" Fiona sat on the floor in front of her mother, who was rocking in an old chair and knitting.

"Really? Sounds a bit interesting," Mother said as she smiled down at her oldest child. "You look excited about it. Is there a bus that will get you home in time for supper?"

"Yes, I checked today on the way home. There is another run at five. Oh, thank you, Mum!" Fiona jumped up and hugged her mother tightly.

"Be careful now, or you'll get jabbed with one of these knitting needles!" her mother said, gently pushing her daughter away. She shook her head and muttered to herself; Fiona ran into her room to make up some dance steps.

The next day after school, Fiona went to the gym. She changed her clothes in the locker room and waited. Several girls whom Fiona recognized gathered in the gym. Charlotte, who was older, leaned against the wall looking glum. She lived with her aunt and uncle since her parents were killed in an auto accident. She almost never talked to anyone. Caroline was there, too. When Fiona had her own group of friends in primary school, they didn't speak to Caroline, although Fiona didn't know why. Caroline did appear angry a lot; perhaps that was the reason. And there were Lara and Jaime, two trouble-makers whom most students avoided. Fiona was surprised that they would like to dance. The others Fiona did not know.

Mrs. McCrary came into the gym. "All right, girls!" she said, clapping her hands together. "Let's do our stretches and then get dancing!" Fiona was amazed at how well the girls could stretch. After years of formal training, Fiona was known for being very flexible; some of these girls almost equaled her. After a few minutes, Mrs. McCrary clapped her hands again. "Are you ready to do our special dance? Let's show Fiona how it's done!" The girls, about eight of them, enthusiastically took their places facing Mrs. McCrary. "Now watch us, Miss Fiona!" she said, and then Mrs. McCrary, the middle-aged gym teacher, danced!

Fiona could see this woman was enjoying herself as she bounded about, but she was obviously not a trained dancer. It didn't seem to matter to the girls. "Jaime, no spikey fingers!" Mrs. McCrary said, and the girls giggled. They followed her moves with similar ones of their own; then Mrs. McCrary hesitated for a second and said, "Now . . . let's add a leap!" She did, and so did they. Then everyone laughed and collapsed to the gym floor. Fiona had never seen such a dance, and hysterical laughter was certainly not something they did in her formal dance classes. She wanted to try it.

"Will you do it again?" she asked Mrs. McCrary.

"Of course!" was the reply. "This time you join us!"

"Okay, girls, try to all stay together, and remember to start to the right . . . or left, whichever you prefer!" instructed Mrs. McCrary. The girls giggled again. Fiona took a place directly in front of Mrs. McCrary. She glanced around quickly at the other girls to see how much room she would have to move. She took a breath; they began. The steps were easy ones for Fiona because of her formal training. Watching Mrs. McCrary was not like watching Miss Elizabeth, her ballet teacher. But it was fun! For the first time in several years, Fiona felt light and free. That afternoon, during the times Mrs. McCrary encouraged the girls to make up their own steps, Fiona fairly flew across the gym floor and imaged herself to be a great choreographer. The hour sped by, and she found herself feeling a bit sad when the time was up.

"Thank you for joining us, Fiona," smiled Mrs. McCrary. "Did you enjoy yourself?"

"Oh, yes, very much. Thank you, Mrs. McCrary," replied Fiona.

For five years, Fiona danced with the after-school dance company. They even began to meet during lunchtime several days a week. Although she didn't become close friends with any of the girls in the group, Fiona felt she belonged. Her longing ceased for the friends who abandoned her after her parents' divorce. She smiled frequently. Fiona's mother noticed and often remarked, "You look cheerful lately, Fiona. I'm glad."

The freedom that Fiona was allowed in Mrs. McCrary's dance company gave her joy. As she grew older, Fiona realized that she no longer *needed* to dance, she *loved* it. And she also loved Mrs. McCrary. This giving teacher worked with the dance company without pay, which Fiona had not understood when she was young. Mrs. McCrary did it because she loved the girls, and she loved to dance.

Every girl in the dance company was a misfit in some way. The girls with high grades and close friends never came to dance. It was always girls like lonely Fiona, angry Caroline, and overweight Lara and Jaime. Mrs. McCrary often stood by the gym door and gave hugs when the girls left to go home. It took some of the girls more than a year to approach this warmhearted woman for a hug, but they got around to it. Fiona hugged her right away. Sometimes she hesitated in Mrs. McCrary's arms for a couple of seconds. She would breathe in her smell, a combination of sweat and . . . what? "Joy" is how Fiona later described Mrs. McCrary's scent. *If joy has a smell, that is certainly what it would be like,* she thought. Mrs. McCrary would whisper, "Thank you for being here, sweet girl."

In her formal class, Fiona was excelling. Miss Elizabeth made comments to Fiona like "Fiona, your dancing has changed. Your talent and hard work have always shown, but there is something different. It adds to your expression, your movements. Your dance finally has . . . voice!" Fiona knew what that meant; all dancers sought that "voice," and she had it at last! She was well aware of where she attained that voice. She thought of sharing the fact with Miss Elizabeth, but Fiona didn't think Miss Elizabeth would understand. How could she possibly explain to this perfectionistic teacher that Mrs. Mc-Crary's imperfect methods, laughter and warmth had made the difference? So Fiona simply smiled and said, "Thank you, Miss Elizabeth."

At age 16, Fiona moved with her family to England. That meant leaving Mrs. McCrary, which was the most difficult thing imaginable. Mrs. McCrary planned a special send-off for Fiona on her last day. Fiona feared the good-bye. She wished she could look forward to it, but she could not. After all, it was a loving gesture, very typical of Mrs. McCrary. There would probably be cake and ice cream, perhaps even a gift. As the day approached, Fiona had trouble sleeping at night.

She had been dancing with Miss Elizabeth for 11 years but had known her gym teacher for only five. Why wasn't she feeling sad about leaving Miss Elizabeth? But when Fiona closed her eyes at night, she pictured Mrs. McCrary's smile. She could almost hear Mrs. McCrary's raucous laughter as she lay on the gym floor after a particularly rigorous dance routine.

On her final day at Falkirk Secondary School, Fiona skipped after-school dance. She quickly stuffed her belongings into her bag and ran for the bus stop. When the earlier bus arrived and the door opened, Fiona looked back at the school. As tears came to her eyes, she boarded the bus and took a seat in the very back.

Fiona was startled back to the present as Lorna elbowed her. "Well, what in the world have you been thinking about?" she asked Fiona. "Your eyes were closed, and you had a smile as wide as the sea we're crossing."

Fiona looked at her friend, not quite seeing her yet. She closed her eyes once more. There she was again, two nights ago, taking a bow on center stage at Carnegie Hall. Flowers were thrown to her, landing at her feet. She stood, and one of the show's producers walked across the stage and handed her a huge bouquet of roses. They filled her arms; she mouthed the words "Thank you" to him. And as her heart swelled with gratitude, Fiona took another bow and thought, *Thank you, Mrs. McCrary. Thank you.*

	LET'S TALK ABOUT IT
1	What feelings do you think Fiona had when her parents got divorced?
2	Who were the bucketfillers in this story? Discuss how they filled buckets.
3	Who were the bucketdippers in this story? Discuss how they dipped into buckets.
4	What kind of a person was Mrs. McCrary? How did she fill buckets? How many buckets do you think she filled as a teacher?
5	What do you think was the most important thing Fiona learned from Mrs. McCrary?
6	Do you have anyone in your life like Mrs. McCrary? If yes, who, and how do you feel about that person?

About the Author

Stacey A. Lundgren happily describes her life as "eclectic." She grew up in and around Chicago, where her family moved often. This early experience taught Stacey to appreciate that there are good people everywhere, and making new friends is easy. The moves also helped her develop a great appreciation and desire for adventure. Her childhood passions included writing and riding horses.

Stacey has lived her adult life in Michigan, Wyoming, Utah, and Alaska. Each place provided her with different adventures. Her favorite adventures include riding horses, working cattle, doctoring cattle, spending time alone in the Alaskan wilderness, and doing some hair-raising flying with Alaskan bush pilots. She describes those flights over the mountains, landing on the ocean and on inland lakes, as "so thrilling and beautiful that they brought tears to my eyes."

Stacey has five children who came into her life in two distinct phases. Her first two were her own birth children. She was thrilled and proud to be able to be a stay-at-home mom with them. After her daughter and son were grown and on their own, Stacey adopted three Bulgarian orphans. She says of this experience, "This was definitely the most challenging, but gratifying adventure of my life!" She is currently a single parent and lives at home in Michigan with her youngest child.

As the co-owner of Bucketfillers For Life, Inc., a Michigan-based character education company, Stacey has presented assemblies and workshops in hundreds of schools for thousands of children, teachers, and administrators. She is available nationally and internationally for keynote addresses, seminars, and teacher/school administrator training programs.

You can learn more about the work and programs of Bucketfillers For Life, Inc., at their website, www.bucketfillersforlife.com

You can contact Ms. Lundgren through Bucketfillers For Life, Inc. or:

By phone or email at:
517-376-3090
info@peacemountainpublishing.com